Attainment's Whole Brain workouts

MARGE ENGELMAN

Whole Brain Workouts

By Marge Engelman

Edited by Elizabeth Ragsdale and Tom Kinney

Graphic design by Elizabeth Ragsdale

Photography by Beverly Potts

ISBN: 1-57861-589-5

An Attainment Publication

Attainment Company, Inc.

PO Box 930160

Verona, WI 53593-0160

1-800-327-4269

www.AttainmentCompany.com

contents

about the author

Marge Engelman has been studying and teaching in the field of "learning in the older years" for over 30 years. Her original research focused on encouraging the creative impulse in aging women.

She has a BA in Sociology, MA in Religious Education, MS in Environmental Design, and PhD in Adult Education. She has developed and taught "Aerobics of the Mind" and "Creativity in Aging" to groups in retirement centers, senior centers and adult daycare centers, and in workshops for leaders of these centers. She has lectured throughout Wisconsin and at national meetings on topics related to learning in the later years. She has taught in the Graduate School of Education at the University of Wisconsin-Madison. She was a Governor's delegate from the state of Wisconsin to the White House Conference on Aging in 1995.

Marge is 78 years old and keeps her own mind active by auditing classes at the University of Wisconsin-Madison, designing innovative textile projects, growing gourds and developing them into works of art, and writing this book.

Comments, questions and reactions to the text are welcomed:

Marge Engelman
738 Seneca Place
Madison, WI 53711
email: engelman@wisc.edu

preface

The workouts in this book are for healthy older adults. The 125 exercises aim to apply what researchers are learning about the brain.

It's now accepted knowledge that stimulation of the brain through many kinds of mental exercise produces a thicker cortex, more neurons and dendrites, and stronger synapses. It's believed that the more mentally fit a brain, the longer it may be able to thrive and resist decline. How we use our brains has a great deal to do with how we age!

The workouts can be used by individuals in everyday life. If you live alone, you may want to do some of the exercises and then compare notes via phone or email with another person who's doing them.

You may want to do these exercises with your spouse, adult children or other relatives and friends. Some are appropriate to do with your grandchildren.

Activity directors will find many of the activities ideal for adult groups in senior centers, retirement homes, churches and other social settings.

Caregivers, whether in the home or in more formal settings, will find the workouts helpful to use with those in their care.

A new profession—mental fitness coaching—is peeking around the corner. Persons doing this coaching will find these exercises invaluable.

acknowledgments

When I began thinking and talking about what I first called "aerobics of the mind," not many people were aware that mental activity is necessary to keep the brain healthy. We were only beginning to understand that the brain is pliable and can continue to change and grow even into old age. But some older adults in senior centers and retirement homes were brave enough to experiment with me and profited from this new way of doing and thinking. They were the fuel that fed my fire for mental fitness. I thank them all, even those who were skeptical.

I am grateful to Venture Publishing at Pennsylvania State University, who published my first book, *Aerobics of the Mind,* in 1996. Later as I searched for a publisher to turn the mental exercises in the book into a set of 100 Mental Fitness Cards, I discovered Don Bastian, CEO of Attainment Company in Verona, Wisconsin. He'd become convinced that providing books, cards, DVDs and other products for the aging population was an important contribution his company could make. We were off and running!

The staff at Attainment have been, without exception, helpful and supportive. I'm especially grateful to Sherri Erickson, who facilitated endless details; Elizabeth Ragsdale, my creative and capable editor; Jo Reynolds, Art Director, who gave insightful suggestions for the design of the book; and Tom Kinney, Vice President of Publishing, who lent his expertise along the way.

I'm grateful to Ken, my husband, who has a healthier brain because he was willing to read and reread the text as it developed and was nudged into trying many of the exercises.

My daughter, Ann Engelman Yocom, questioned, encouraged, listened and supported me as I thrashed out ideas. Kari Berit Gustafson, a former student and now a colleague with her own business, Age in Motion, is a continuing inspiration.

ONE

getting started

Most people now understand that a healthy lifestyle includes physical fitness. But in the last few years we've learned that brain fitness is equally important. It's possible to work out our minds just as we work out our bodies. The results can be improved memory, clearer thinking, a more positive attitude and a healthier lifestyle.

One of the biggest myths about aging is that our brain power diminishes as we grow older. Brain function may slow down, but most of the decline isn't because of aging. It's often because we neglect to challenge the brain.

Challenge is as essential for the brain as movement is for the muscles. Intellectual stimulation and enrichment actually cause structural changes in the brain. The small branches (dendrites) of brain cells (neurons) sprout new branches when the brain is challenged. When parts of the brain are stimulated by certain life tasks and mental exercise, more blood goes to those areas and new dendrites and connections are formed.

What about the neurons and the dendrites?

The brain, which weighs about three pounds, is made up of over 100 billion neurons. A neuron may interact with thousands of other cells, some of them quite far away. The cell body of a neuron contains separate sets of tubular sending and receiving extensions, called axons and dendrites. The dendrites have tiny spines. The synapses, or contact points between these spines, are both electrical and chemical. This drawing helps visualize how neurons work.

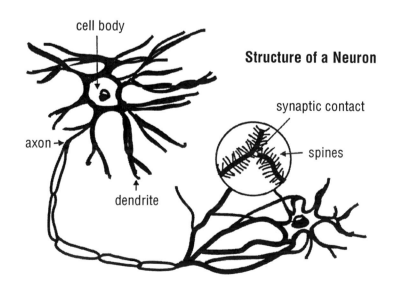

cell body

Structure of a Neuron

synaptic contact

axon →

← spines

↑
dendrite

It's said that the brain is the most complicated piece of equipment in the universe. To understand its complexity it's helpful to know these facts:

• Thirty thousand neurons can fit into a space the size of a pinhead.
• The brain has the information processing power of a hundred billion medium-sized computers.
• There are more neurons in the brain than there are stars in the milky way.
• The normal brain has a quadrillion connections between the cells, more than all the phone calls made in the United States in the past decade.

Left brain/right brain

We sometimes refer to a person as right-brained or left-brained. The assumption is that a right-brain person is generally creative, intuitive, artsy and fond of color. A left-brain person is thought to be linear, logical, adept at problem solving and good with numbers.

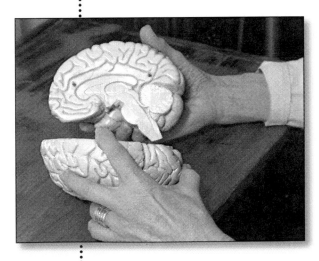

Recent brain scan technology, however, shows that the functions of the left and right hemispheres of the brain are not quite so cut and dried. It's now thought that the two sides are more interdependent. For example, language processing, once believed to be left hemisphere-only, is now understood to take place in both hemispheres: The left side processes grammar and pronunciation, while the right processes intonation.

As we continue to learn more about the brain, we're sure to find that this miracle that sits atop each of our bodies is more complicated than we once thought.

New discoveries about the brain will continue to be made for many years to come. Thus we cannot say with assurance that we know exactly what the exercises in this book will accomplish. But in general, we're quite sure that doing a variety of mental exercises will foster a healthy brain.

How much of our brains do we use?

An old myth held that we use only a small percentage of our brain, perhaps 10 percent. We now know that we use virtually all of our brain every day. Brain imaging techniques, such as positron emission tomography (PET) and functional magnetic resonance imaging (fMRI), allow scientists to see the brain in action.

By detecting areas of blood flow, associated with neuron activity, imaging can identify which parts of the brain are active under different conditions. For example, if you were munching on a sandwich while reading this page, the frontal lobes in your cerebral cortex would be engaged in thinking and reasoning. You would be enjoying your sandwich thanks to your parietal lobes, which are responsible for taste, texture and smell. The occipital lobes would help you process the words you see on this page, and the temporal lobes would help you process the crunch of the sandwich and the rustle of the paper you hear.

The following diagram of the brain shows which areas are responsible for various functions.

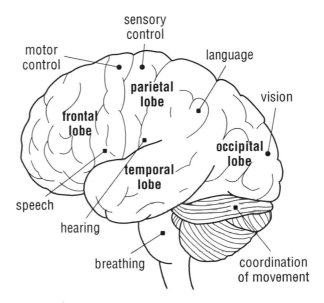

Functions of the Brain

What happens to our minds as we age?

Researchers have found that some cognitive decline does occur prior to the age of 60. When we reach our 80s almost everyone has some decline in mental function. But from our 60s to 80s how much our mental ability slips really depends on a lot of things, some of which are under our control.

Diseases that rise dramatically in incidence with age—such as mild cognitive impairment, Alzheimer's, Parkinson's and depression—have their roots in brain health. The well-being of the brain also affects most other issues of aging, including mobility, autonomy and living with dignity.

It's clear that healthy aging must include keeping our minds active. As Will Rogers said, "You know you've got to exercise your brain just like your muscles."

What can we control?

We can control a number of factors in our lives, such as physical exercise, a healthy diet, socialization with others. These are all important to a healthy lifestyle, but here we will focus on a broad range of brain workouts, which are a key factor in a positive quality of life.

Continuing to learn is one of the most powerful activities for stimulating the brain. Seeking out activities that require thinking and decision making are important. Doing things new and different for you is highly desirable. The brain thrives on novelty.

The workouts in this book are designed to help you take control of your mental fitness.

How much mental exercise is enough?

We don't have a tried and proven curriculum yet, but research on mental exercise is progressing that will help us know what kind, how much and how often. Because everyone's different, there's no one-size-fits-all workout plan.

A variety of guesses have been made about how much mental exercise is enough. The day is coming when we'll be able to pinpoint a weakened part of the brain and then recommend workouts to facilitate rejuvenation. This process is called neurogenesis, a breakthrough concept in our understanding of the aging brain.

In the meantime, basic research informs us that doing a variety of activities and exercises will strengthen our mental abilities. A glance at the contents of this book will give you a clue about the wide range of activities likely to be helpful. Like the body, the brain needs a balance of workouts.

What about watching TV?

The most common mistake older people make regarding mental activity is to watch too much TV. The average person watches about four hours daily. TV provides us with a great deal of information and entertainment, but most programs allow the brain to be passive, thus eroding mental abilities.

Reading

On the other hand, many neurological researchers believe reading is uniquely beneficial for the brain. Reading requires active engagement of the mind and imagination, and it powerfully stimulates both hemispheres of the brain. Reading is to the brain what physical exercise is to the body. Reading out loud is especially beneficial.

Evaluating your mental fitness

How mentally fit is your brain? The Mental Fitness Evaluation Form, which begins on the following page, will help you think about the factors that make for a healthy brain.

So often we think of the big M (memory) as the major factor of a healthy mind. Actually, many components contribute to mental fitness. Doing this evaluation will help you realize the variety of activities that help build your mental muscle.

After you've finished the evaluation form, review the items in which you checked "Seldom" or "Once in awhile." Make a list of these areas that probably could use some extra attention. As you do the brain workouts in this book, pay special heed to those suggested activities that will stretch your brainpower in these areas.

Mental Fitness Evaluation Form

1. How often during the day do you take time to do some deep breathing?

    ☐ Seldom ☐ Once in awhile ☐ Often ☐ Always

2. How often do you deliberately try to do something new and different for you?

    ☐ Seldom ☐ Once in awhile ☐ Often ☐ Always

3. How often do you find things to laugh about?

    ☐ Seldom ☐ Once in awhile ☐ Often ☐ Always

4. How often do you memorize phone numbers, license numbers, a famous quote or a poem?

    ☐ Seldom ☐ Once in awhile ☐ Often ☐ Always

5. Are you involved in activities that challenge your creativity?

    ☐ Seldom ☐ Once in awhile ☐ Often ☐ Always

6. Do you ever do word games such as crossword puzzles, Jumbles, Scrabble?

    ☐ Seldom ☐ Once in awhile ☐ Often ☐ Always

7. Do you read a newspaper or magazines?

    ☐ Seldom ☐ Once in awhile ☐ Often ☐ Always

8. Do you work with mathematics, numbers, logic problems?

    ☐ Seldom ☐ Once in awhile ☐ Often ☐ Always

9. Do you take time for a hobby you enjoy?

☐ Seldom ☐ Once in awhile ☐ Often ☐ Always

10. Do you ever do jigsaw puzzles?

☐ Seldom ☐ Once in awhile ☐ Often ☐ Always

11. Do you play a musical instrument?

☐ Seldom ☐ Once in awhile ☐ Often ☐ Always

12. Do you write in a diary or write letters to family and friends?

☐ Seldom ☐ Once in awhile ☐ Often ☐ Always

13. Are you able to visualize the route to walk or drive when someone gives you directions?

☐ Seldom ☐ Once in awhile ☐ Often ☐ Always

14. Do you ever play board games with other people?

☐ Seldom ☐ Once in awhile ☐ Often ☐ Always

15. Are you good at remembering people's names?

☐ Seldom ☐ Once in awhile ☐ Often ☐ Always

16. Do you delight in remembering things that happened a long time ago?

☐ Seldom ☐ Once in awhile ☐ Often ☐ Always

17. Are you good at making decisions when you go shopping?

☐ Seldom ☐ Once in awhile ☐ Often ☐ Always

18. Are you able to "be in charge of your life"?

☐ Seldom ☐ Once in awhile ☐ Often ☐ Always

TWO

whole brain workouts

More than twice as many Americans (62%) fear losing their mental capacity with age as those who fear losing their physical capacity (29%). Lessening that fear is a goal of these brain workouts.

Just as a good physical workout exercises many parts of the body, these mental exercises provide stimulation for many parts of the brain.

Because the brain is a miracle of complexity, attempting to stimulate one part will inevitably stimulate other parts of the brain as well. However, research gives us good reason to believe that zeroing in on certain areas will have noticeable benefits.

These model workouts draw exercises from different chapters of the book. Be sure to try ALL of the exercises suggested in any one workout as a way to stimulate multiple parts of the brain.

Resist the temptation to do only those exercises that you like and are easy for you. Trying to do a difficult exercise is a valuable workout too. For example, if you don't like numbers, be sure to try Sudoku, a unique number game that promises to sharpen your ability to reason. Even if you don't finish the grid, you'll stretch your mental muscles.

Beginning the workouts

We typically breath effortlessly and automatically—nearly 20,000 times a day—thanks mainly to our lungs. But most of us older adults are notoriously shallow breathers. We need to breathe more deliberately, slowly, deeply. Practice the following breathing exercise advocated by Dr. Andrew Weil. You can do the exercise sitting with your back straight, lying on your back, or standing or walking.

> Exhale completely through your mouth, making an audible sound. Then, close your mouth and inhale quietly through your nose to a count of four. Hold your breath for a count of seven. Next exhale audibly through your mouth to a count of eight. Repeat for a total of four cycles, and then breathe normally.

The speed with which you do the exercise is unimportant. What's important is the ratio of four, seven and eight for inhalation, hold and exhalation.

Be sure to follow this breathing routine at the start of a workout. Repeat three or four times for optimum benefit.

A place and time

Setting aside a specific time and place to practice brain workouts can be helpful. Just as you may have special equipment for doing physical exercise, it can be helpful to have a special place where you regularly do your brain workouts. Be sure to have paper and pencil at hand.

In planning when to do mental exercises, habit can be a powerful force. By establishing a pattern of doing the exercises at a certain time of day, you'll reinforce your practice. Of course, many of the exercises can be done anytime, but just as some people start their day with a crossword puzzle, you could determine to do brain workouts at the same time each day. (Think about doing some of these exercises while you work out at the gym.)

The point is to be DELIBERATE. Decide that brain workouts deserve to be a priority in your life. It'll pay off!

Amount of time spent working out

It would be good to plan on at least 15–20 minutes for each workout. Some exercises will take longer than others. There are no time limits, so don't feel hurried.

You'll find that some of the workouts are suggestions of places to go or things to think about rather than doing an exercise that requires you to be in one place.

For example, Exercise 4 suggests you go where kids are playing and join in their fun, and Exercise 5 suggests you go to a party store. This kind of variety may help you feel like you're "getting out of the gym." Play hooky and live it up!

Frequency of workouts

Doing workouts every day would be wonderful. At the least, try to do a full workout three times a week. The more often you do the exercises, the more agile your brain becomes. You'll surprise yourself in how brain-smart you really are. And you'll add zest to your life.

The Whole Brain Workout Planner

A good motto might be: "A workout a day keeps the cobwebs away."

First, find the specific exercises in Workout 1 of the Whole Brain Workout Planner on the next page. Make a serious effort to do what's suggested.

When you've finished an exercise, check it off on the Workout Planner. Then go on to the next exercise, checking it off when you've finished. Continue until all five exercises are completed in Workout 1.

After you've tried some workouts in the Planner and have an idea of the variety of exercises included, you can put together your own workouts. Begin by photocopying the blank Workout Planner on page 26. For each workout be sure to select exercises from a variety of chapters in this book.

There are no absolute guarantees of what these exercises will do for you. But there's a good chance you'll feel sharper, your memory will be better and in general you'll feel healthier.

WHOLE BRAIN WORKOUT PLANNER

Name _____ Date _____

Chapter	Workout 1	Workout 2	Workout 3	Workout 4	Workout 5	Workout 6
Chapter 3 Laughter Is Good for the Brain		Exercise 1 Page 32		Exercise 5 Page 35		Exercise 7 Page 36
Chapter 4 Sharpen Your Memory	Exercise 16 Page 48		Exercise 18 Page 49		Exercise 21 Page 52	
Chapter 5 Free Your Creativity and Imagination		Exercise 26 Page 58		Exercise 28 Page 60	Exercise 32 Page 64	
Chapter 6 Words, Words, Words		Exercise 44 Page 80	Exercise 47 Page 82			Exercise 51 Page 84
Chapter 7 Power Up Your Mind with Puzzles and Numbers	Exercise 61 Page 96		Exercise 63 Page 98		Exercise 66 Page 101	
Chapter 8 Strengthen Your Sense of Smell and Taste		Exercise 69 Page 106		Exercise 71 Page 107		Exercise 75 Page 110
Chapter 9 Have Fun with Visual Arts and Illusions	Exercise 77 Page 112			Exercise 80 Page 116		
Chapter 10 Build Your Spatial Abilities		Exercise 88 Page 124			Exercise 91 Page 126	
Chapter 11 Remember When	Exercise 97 Page 132		Exercise 101 Page 134			Exercise 104 Page 136
Chapter 12 Games Make Brains			Exercise 115 Page 147		Exercise 117 Page 148	
Chapter 13 Television and Computers	Exercise 122 Page 152			Exercise 123 Page 153		Exercise 124 Page 153

WHOLE BRAIN WORKOUT PLANNER

Name _____   Date _____

	Workout 1	Workout 2	Workout 3	Workout 4	Workout 5	Workout 6
Chapter 3 Laughter Is Good for the Brain						
Chapter 4 Sharpen Your Memory						
Chapter 5 Free Your Creativity and Imagination						
Chapter 6 Words, Words, Words						
Chapter 7 Power Up Your Mind with Puzzles and Numbers						
Chapter 8 Strengthen Your Sense of Smell and Taste						
Chapter 9 Have Fun with Visual Arts and Illusions						
Chapter 10 Build Your Spatial Abilities						
Chapter 11 Remember When						
Chapter 12 Games Make Brains						
Chapter 13 Television and Computers						

Using whole brain workouts with a group

A group could be 3–4 people or 5–15 people, but a larger group is usually more challenging. Here are suggested guidelines for using these workouts in a group setting.

The physical setting

The ideal arrangement is for the participants to sit around a table so that everyone can see the facilitator and each other. Each person should have a comfortable chair. Adequate lighting and a quiet setting with a minimum of noise are also important.

A chalkboard or flip chart and paper and pencils are basic equipment. Other items needed will become evident in the specific exercises.

The facilitator

A good facilitator has these qualities:

- Displays a warm and caring attitude in helping each person feel welcome and shows genuine interest in each participant.
- Learns everyone's name as soon as possible and encourages others to learn the names of the group members.
- Shows enthusiasm for the workout activities.
- Learns from participants and is open to their suggestions.

- Encourages persons to speak, but is diplomatic in setting limits if someone tends to dominate (see Ground Rules for Discussion on page 29).
- Shows a sense of humor and encourages others in contributing humor.
- Finds ways to encourage persons who are hesitant to participate.
- Demonstrates sensitivity to how much participants can do comfortably.
- Asks for feedback at the end of a session, seeking out what participants liked and what they wished had been different.

The author, earlier in her career, leads a group of women striving to increase their creative abilities.

Ground rules for discussion

Establishing and following a few basic ground rules will make the activities more pleasant for all:

- Each person's opinion counts.
- Everyone participates; no one dominates.
- One speaks; others listen.
- It's okay to disagree, but not to be disagreeable.
- Speak positively.
- Stay focused.
- Begin and end on time.

Special tips

Often one or more persons in a group will have a hearing problem or will have trouble seeing or writing. These disabilities should not dampen energy for doing these brain workouts. Members of the group can help each other, or perhaps an aide can support the person who needs help hearing, seeing or writing.

You will not find timed exercises here. We've been brainwashed to believe faster is better. Time pressure may have a small place in some exercises, but in general we need to give permission for participants to go at their own speed. Pressure usually creates stress, and stress is not the name of the game here.

Be sure to encourage group members to be leaders whenever possible. Give some thought to how the group could get along without you. The ultimate compliment to your leadership would be for them to decide they can survive quite well when you're not there.

What workouts to use

You may want to begin with the workouts suggested on page 25. But then feel free to pick and choose from the 125 exercises in this book, remembering the importance of choosing exercises from a variety of chapters in an effort to stretch many parts of the brain.

THREE

laughter is good for the brain

Patch Adams, MD, has written a delightful and informative book, *Gesundheit!* The book focuses on the importance of humor in our daily lives. Wearing a red, bulbous rubber nose wherever he goes, he tries to make his own life silly. "Silly," he says, "means good, happy, blessed, fortunate and cheerful in many different languages."

Patch Adams is convinced that laughter has a positive physical effect on the brain as well as many other organs of our body. He declares that, psychologically, humor forms the foundation of good mental health.

Do you remember that the late Norman Cousins wrote about having laughed himself back to health after suffering a serious chronic disease?

The experience had such an impact on him that he changed careers late in life to bring this information to health care professionals.

Laughter improves blood circulation, exercises abdominal muscles, increases heart rate, expels stale air from lungs, aids digestion and releases muscle tension. After a round of laughter, blood pressure drops to a lower, healthier level.

In an Apache myth the Creator gives human beings the ability to talk, to run and to look. But the Creator is not satisfied until people also have the ability to laugh. Only then does the Creator say, "Now you are fit to live."

Knock-knock jokes

Remember the knock-knock jokes of our childhood days that we used to try out on our friends and family? They were often quite silly, but fun.

> Knock, knock. Who's there? Justin. Justin who?
> Justin time for dinner.

Here are a few more to stretch your brain and add some laughs to your day. Make up your own answers and then check the answers in Appendix A. Be sure not to look until you've tried to answer all of the knock-knocks.

1. Knock, knock. Who's there? Goliath. Goliath who?

_____

2. Knock, knock. Who's there? Dewayne. Dewayne who?

_____

3. Knock, knock. Who's there? Freeze. Freeze who?

_____

4. Knock, knock. Who's there? Isabelle. Isabelle who?

_____

5. Knock, knock. Who's there? Butter. Butter who?

_____

Now for the real challenge. Invent some of your own knock-knocks, and then try them on whoever will listen.

2 More knock-knocks

1. Knock, knock. Who's there? Amanda. Amanda who?

_____

2. Knock, knock. Who's there? Toby? Toby who?

_____

3. Knock, knock. Who's there? Offer. Offer Who?

_____

4. Knock, knock. Who's there? Dawn. Dawn who?

_____

5. Knock, knock. Who's there? Nunya. Nunya who?

_____

6. Knock, knock. Who's there? Disease. Disease who?

_____

Continue to develop some of your own knock-knocks, and try not to antagonize too many people.

3   Comics of the past and present

Remember comics such as Charlie Chaplin, Buster Keaton, the Marx Brothers, the Three Stooges, Abbott and Costello, Lucille Ball, Red Skelton, Carol Burnett, Woody Allen, Lily Tomlin, Pee-Wee Herman?

Your challenge for several days is to look for videos of these stand-up comics. Pick your favorites and set aside some time to replay their antics and laugh up a gale.

In spite of the number of people who have claimed to have done so, no one has ever died laughing. Maybe if we could keep the hilarity rolling we could all live forever.

4 Little children

Little children are naturally funny. Find a way to go where kids are and join in their play. They'll be delighted that you would want to play with them.

5 Visit a party store

Throw a party! Make it a party that allows you to be crazy and have fun. It won't cost much and the laughter you'll generate is invaluable. Visit a party store for inspiration.

Party stores carry a variety of items that encourage you to be silly. Look for eyeglasses with a nose and mustache, clacking teeth, wigs, feather boas and noise makers.

Hats are one of the best ways to have fun. Try a discarded lampshade for starters. Suspenders can encourage you to strut your stuff. Huge earrings can turn you into a party girl. It wouldn't cost you anything to wear your underwear on the outside of your clothes. Wear wild colors and patterns that don't go together.

You're probably asking, But what will people think? You're thinking you'd be embarrassed. At our age, we can get away with it, especially during a private party. Think of the good laughs that will result. And good laughs add jest to your life.

Shout yippee! Giggle! Smile! Make sure you celebrate.

A dozen ways to add fun to your life

1. Try to come up with a more distinctive signature.
2. Test drive a car you'd probably never buy.
3. Contact an old friend from your faraway past.
4. Record a new message on your answering machine such as "Hello? Hello? Is anybody there?" or sing a tune instead of speaking.
5. Try a vegetable or fruit that's new to you such as kale, arugula, a cherimoya or a papaya.
6. Stick some bottle caps on the soles of an old pair of shoes, and tap dance on a hard surface.
7. Drink a bottle of soda and have a burping contest with a friend.
8. Buy a bottle of liquid bubbles and blow bubbles with a friend, a neighbor child or your pet.
9. Blow on dandelions and spread the seeds far and wide.
10. Eat lunch at a place you have walked by many times but never tried.
11. Teach yourself to play the spoons.
12. Collect wind-up toys.

Brain teasers

Stretch your brain with these brain teasers. Try first to write the answer to each one, and check Appendix A only after you've puzzled over all the questions.

1. What in an automobile engine serves no purpose, but without it the engine does not work? _____

   _____

2. You have a dime and a dollar. You buy a dog and a collar. The dog costs a dollar more than the collar. How much is the collar? _____

   _____

3. On my way to the fair, I met 7 jugglers and a bear. Every juggler had 6 cats; every cat had 5 rats; every rat had 4 houses; every house had 3 mice; every mouse had a louse and its spouse. How many in all are going to the fair? _____

   _____

4. Imagine you're in a sinking rowboat surrounded by sharks. How would you survive? _____

   _____

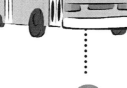

5. You're driving a bus. Four people get on and 3 people get off; then 8 people get on and 10 people get off; then 6 people get on and 2 more people get off. What color were the bus driver's eyes? _____

   _____

8 More brain teasers

Write your answers to these brain teasers. After you've tried your best to answer them, check Appendix A. Be sure to try! Trying stimulates your brain cells.

1. A man left home running. He ran a ways and then turned left, ran the same distance and turned left again, ran the same distance and turned left again. When he got home there were two masked men there. Who were they? _____

   _____

2. There was an airplane crash. Every single person died, but two people survived. How is this possible? _____

   _____

3 Peacocks are birds that do not lay eggs. How do they get baby peacocks? _____

   _____

4. Eskimos are very good hunters, but they never hunt penguins. Why not? _____

   _____

5. A man and his son were in an automobile accident. The man died on the way to the hospital, but the boy was rushed into surgery. The emergency room surgeon said, "I can't operate, that's my son!" How is that possible? _____

   _____

6. What came first, the chicken or the egg? _____

   _____

Like puns?

Each sentence below makes sense (or at least nonsense) if you insert one of these flower names:

heather	crocus	mimosa	poppy
hyacinth	zinnia	daisy	jonquil
lilac	wisteria	dahlia	

For example: If you insert ASTER in "I _____ to go out for a drive," it makes sense, right?

1. Riding the merry-go-round makes me _____.

2. He can _____ a trooper.

3. It doesn't bother _____ the time.

4. He keeps pushing me _____ and yon.

5. I'll bet you a _____ you're wrong.

6. Do you think he's planning to _____?

7. I know where my Mommy is but I can't find my _____.

8. It's just a bad case of _____.

9. Everything is _____ war started again.

10. That pile of _____ only rust if you leave it there.

11. So long, I'll be _____.

10 Humorous captions

Write three humorous captions for the image below.

1. _____

   _____

2. _____

   _____

3. _____

   _____

11 More humorous captions

Write five humorous captions for the image below.

1. _____

_____

2. _____

_____

3. _____

_____

4. _____

_____

5. _____

_____

12 An unusual cat

Take your time and see if you can read each line aloud without a mistake. (The average person cannot.)

This is this cat
This is is cat
This is how cat
This is to cat
This is keep cat
This is an cat
This is older cat
This is person cat
This is busy cat
This is for cat
This is twenty cat
This is seconds cat.

Now go back and read the third word in each line from the top down.

Are you surprised? For an even better exercise for your brain, compose a new "poem," using the same principle, but different words.

13 Laugh and live

The average child laughs hundreds of times a day.
The average adult laughs only a dozen times a day.

Try these one-liners to raise your laughter quotient:

- A bicycle can't stand alone because it's two-tired.
- When a clock is hungry it goes back four seconds.
- A lot of money is tainted. 'Taint yours and 'taint mine.
- He had a photographic memory that was never developed.
- You feel stuck with your debt if you can't budge it.
- Those who get too big for their britches will be exposed in the end.
- When you have seen one shopping center you've see a mall.
- Those who jump off a Paris bridge are in Seine.
- Acupuncture is a jab well done.

Feeling a little bit healthier? Using this model, can you come up with some funnies of your own?

How do you catch a unique rabbit?

- How do you catch a unique rabbit? **Unique up on it.**
- How do you catch a tame rabbit? **Tame way, unique up on it.**
- What do Eskimos get from sitting on the ice too long? **Polaroids.**
- What do you get from a pampered cow? **Spoiled milk.**
- What do you get when you cross a snowman with a vampire? **Frostbite.**
- What lies at the bottom of the ocean and twitches? **A nervous wreck.**
- What's the difference between roast beef and pea soup? **Anyone can roast beef.**
- Why do gorillas have big nostrils? **Because they have big fingers.**

- What kind of coffee was served on the Titanic? **Sanka.**
- Why did pilgrims' pants always fall down? **Because they wore their belt buckle on their hat.**

How many of these made you smile, maybe even laugh?

15 Know a good joke?

Many of us know a good joke or two. Some folks tell the same jokes over and over. Here are several new ones for your mental file. Try to remember them and share them with someone.

- A man was telling his neighbor, "I just bought a new hearing aid. It cost me $4,000, but it's state of the art. It's perfect."

  "Really," answered the neighbor. " What kind is it?"

  "Twelve thirty."

- A man shuffled slowly into an ice cream parlor and pulled himself slowly, painfully, up onto a stool. After catching his breath he ordered a banana split. The waitress asked kindly, "Crushed nuts?" "No," he replied, "arthritis."

- Did you hear about the robbery at the police station? Thieves broke in and stole all the toilets. The police have nothing to go on.

- Lillian and George were an older couple who had been dating now and then. Both had lost their spouses and they enjoyed each other's company. Sometimes they went to a movie; sometimes they went for a ride in the country. One evening when George was eating a meal at Lillian's home, he thought to himself, "I'll ask her to marry me." So he asked her and she said yes. But on the way home George started thinking, "Did she say yes or did she say no?" He was so upset with himself he hardly slept that night. He arose early the next morning and phoned Lillian and said, "I'm so sorry, Lillian, I can't remember if you said yes, or no." There was an audible sigh of relief and Lillian responded saying, "Oh, I'm so glad you called, I couldn't remember who asked me."

Now recall a joke you know. Write it down and then share it with someone.

sharpen your memory

Most of us aren't accurate judges of our memory. Have you visited a kindergarten room recently and checked the lost and found box? You probably found mittens, scarves, boots, lunch boxes, pencils and glasses. Have you gone to a city park and noticed that children have left behind jackets, buckets and shovels in the sand pile, maybe one sock?

On the college campus it's routine for students to forget their notebooks, pens, the latest assignment or a change of rooms where class meets.

Memory lapses occur at all ages, but at different ages people react differently. In kindergarten we expect it; college students find their forgetfulness amusing, or at the worst annoying, but it's no big deal.

But as we age and our memory falters a bit, we react with embarrassment and fear, responding to the false notion that old age causes loss of memory.

Recent studies have shown that most healthy older people retain the same number of facts under the same circumstances as younger people and are just as capable of learning, but at a slower pace.

16 Don't blame your age

We tend to feel that our memory is bad, not so much when it is bad, but when we feel bad. In her excellent book, *Total Memory Workout*, Cynthia Green suggests that many lifestyle factors can lower your memory potential: Lack of physical activity, inadequate diet, insufficient mental activity, vision and hearing problems, loss and grief, alcohol, fatigue, medications, depression, anxiety, stress and information overload.

Take paper and pencil and list the above lifestyle factors. Then thoughtfully check which ones might be creating memory problems for you. Once you've identified which issues are getting in your way, take a step toward concrete action. For example, if you get little physical exercise, you might decide to do some walking every day. If you have a hearing problem, check with your doctor to see if a hearing aid would help. If stress is prominent in your life, you might want to learn to meditate.

Try not to blame memory loss on age without considering other common causes of impaired memory.

17 Pay attention

There are many ways to develop your memory, but one of the most important is to PAY ATTENTION. For example, when you meet someone new, do you concentrate on the person's name, do you say the name out loud several times and perhaps associate it with something that will help you remember?

There are many ways to practice paying attention. One is to focus your attention on everything in the room you are in. With paper and pencil, list every single item in the room, including the light switches and heating vents. You'll be amazed at how long your list is and how many things you've never really "seen."

Here's another valuable exercise: The next time you visit with your doctor, pay close attention to all the doctor says to you. You may want to make notes. It's amazing how easy it is to forget important information unless you're focusing intently.

18 Memorize

What happens as we age isn't that our memory declines, but that we don't exercise our memory. Do you remember that Bob Hope at 94 was still doing his stand-up joke routines? Mark Russell, the political satirist, is 78 years old. He regularly does his half hour show on PBS without notes. How do they do it? They practice! They have honed their memory skills because that's how they make a living.

Most of us have similar capacities if we'd only take the time to practice. When was the last time you made an effort to memorize something?

Search out something right now that you'd like to memorize. It could be a quote you like such as "Be patient with all that is unanswered in your heart and try to love the questions" (Rilke, the poet). Or pick several verses from the Bible, Torah or Koran and make a point of memorizing them. Perhaps there's a popular tune you could memorize.

Do you know your Social Security number? Is there a phone number of a family member or friend that you always look up before you dial? Commit it to memory right now.

Memorization is one of the best ways to keep your brain sharp. Determine to do it!

19 Tip of the tongue

Do you sometimes say: "It's on the tip of my tongue. It's right there. What's her name?"

As we grow older (some say starting at age 30), most of us have tip-of-the-tongue experiences. Somehow we feel we know the word or name, we might even know the letter it begins with or have a mental image, but the word just isn't accessible.

Why does it happen? We're learning that words, numbers and experiences are stored in different parts of the brain. No one seems to know why some memories are more difficult to recall than others, but it may have to do with the complexities of the brain's storage system.

Dr. Warner Schaie, a Pennsylvania State University professor, states that older people can have more troubles remembering because their brain gets more cluttered over time. He says, "Unfortunately our brain doesn't have an erase button." He notes that every day we're adding to our store of information and it becomes more difficult for us to sort things out. Some researchers have labeled this "information overload."

The next time you have a tip-of-the-tongue experience, try to remember to relax and accept the blank spot. The information will come to you in time. As they say, "Not to worry."

20 Memory boosting exercises

"I'm having a senior moment" is not a very helpful saying. Recently a five year old, upon forgetting something, said to his grandmother, "I'm having a kindergarten moment." Right! At all ages we forget.

Memory loss does worry many people, both young and old, because of increased awareness of Alzheimer's. But unless you're forgetting words like fork and spoon, and not remembering what your car keys are used for, you're probably just fine.

Why is it that we always dwell on the things we forget—the name of a person we just met or the location of our wallet or glasses? We don't think about the thousands of things we do remember every day. We have the ability to train our brains; we need to believe in that potential and cultivate it.

A good way to boost your recall is to do memory improvement exercises. Studies of people who received 10 brain-training lessons over a period of six weeks had important improvement in memory, concentration and problem-solving skills.

If possible, purchase or check the library for a book on improving your memory. There are many such books, for example:

- *Improving Your Memory* by Janet Fogler and Lynn Stern
- *Don't Forget* by Danielle C. Lapp
- *Total Memory Workout* by Cynthia Green

Take the time to learn memory techniques. The following exercises give you a glimpse of some of these methods.

21 Association

Instead of making a written list when you go to the grocery store, associate each item you want to purchase with another item. For instance, if you need fish and milk, visualize the fish swimming in the milk. If you need bread and catsup, visualize the bread dripping with catsup. Researchers say that associations involving movement are the most helpful.

Another association technique is to set words to the tune you used to learn the A, B, Cs. Recall the tune and sing it. Now using that same tune, set your grocery list to the music. For instance, replace A—B—C with apples— bread—cabbage.

Why does this work? Music and rhythm tend to be processed in the right brain, while words tend to be processed in the left brain. When you combine the two, learning is reinforced.

22 Name-face recall

Take note of a prominent feature of the person whose name you want to remember. For example, Mr. Newman has large ears. Remember the name Newman by imagining the actor Paul Newman with very large ears. Ms. Stewart has sparkling teeth. Remember her by imagining Martha Stewart scrubbing her teeth. Suppose the name is Hazelton. You might make the association with a ton of hazelnuts.

Write down several names you have difficulty remembering and devise a name-face recall technique.

Researchers at Yale University suggest that when you have trouble remembering a word or a name, look up to the right. The theory is that words and names are usually located in the left side of the brain and that looking up to the right stimulates that part of the brain. Try it—it often works.

23 Chunking

Telephone numbers are spaced out in "chunks." Social Security numbers are divided into three sets of digits or chunks. These divisions are designed to help our brain memorize them more easily.

If you haven't memorized your Social Security number, do it now. Then think of another number you use regularly, such as your bank account number, and devise a chunking scheme that will help you remember it.

24 Eat right

We're learning that what we eat can affect our memory. People who eat an abundance of fish, leafy greens and monounsaturated fats such as olive oil experience less mental decline, while those who load up on saturated fats and trans fats, found in red meats and many store-bought baked items, are at increased risk for mental decline.

Make a chart and keep track of what you eat for two weeks—breakfast, lunch and dinner. You may be surprised that your diet is lacking in brain-healthy foods.

25 Be physically active

Exercise seems to enhance brain performance in three basic ways:

1. It increases the flow of oxygen to the brain and may help build tiny blood vessels that pave the way for the growth of new cells.
2. It boosts substances called growth factors that help the survival of new nerve cells.
3. It increases chemicals in the brain called neurotransmitters, which play a role in cognition.

A study of some 18,000 women aged 70 years and older found that those who walked at a leisurely pace for two to

three hours a week did much better on tests of memory and thinking ability than inactive women. Women who walked at least six hours a week had the cognitive ability of a person three years younger than their actual age.

If you're not a walker, begin by walking a few blocks (or a few lengths of a shopping mall) for a week. Then gradually increase your walking each week until you're sweating a little. Using an exercise machine can give you the same benefits, but for most of us, walking outside in the fresh air is a bonus.

Research is showing that exercise may even help stall the progression of dementias. So without a doubt it's important to exercise for the mental benefits.

FIVE

free your creativity and imagination

Often when we think of mental fitness, the first thing that pops into our minds is the big M. If your memory is good you assume you're mentally fit. If your memory is poor you conclude you're not mentally fit. Not necessarily. What about your ability to solve problems, be creative, use your imagination? These are all important traits of staying sharp.

Albert Einstein said that imagination is more important than knowledge. We expect children to have good imaginations, but somehow as we age, we often lose that wonderful creative power of imagination.

26   Idea finding

The following problems are meant to demonstrate how unconventional uses for a conventional product can be thought up at will. To give your brain a good workout, pick two of the following problems and with paper and pencil list as many ideas as you can. See how creative you can be.

Idea finding

1. Name all the possible uses for a common brick. For example: Bookends, insulator under hot dishes, lamp base, foot warmer. Name at least 10 more uses.

2. List every possible use that might be made of a brush of the size and kind usually used for painting a house.

3. Write the title of the last movie you saw. Now suggest three other titles you think could have been chosen.

4. Name five inventions the world could use to advantage, but which have not been invented.

27 More idea finding

Pick two of the following problems and write all the ideas that come to you to solve the problem. After you think you have thought of every possible answer, press yourself to come up with several more ideas.

More idea finding

1. What improvements in a bus would you suggest for the comfort and convenience of passengers?

2. Write five imaginary headlines you would most like to see in tomorrow morning's paper.

3. List all the words, phrases and figures of speech, including slang, that you can think of which might be used instead of the word "absurd."

4. List 15 uses for old magazines.

5. You have been asked to give the sermon next week at your church. Think of six possible topics on which you can speak.

28 Creative problem solving

Here's a story to inspire you:

> An old German lived close to New York City for more than 40 years. He loved to plant potatoes in his garden, but he was getting old and weak. His son was in college in London, so the old man sent him an email explaining the problem: "I am very sad because I can't plant potatoes in my garden this year. I am sure that if only you were here you would help me and dig up the garden for me. Love, Your Father."
>
> The following day the old man received an email response from his son: "My father, please don't touch the garden. It's there that I have hidden 'THE THING.' Love, Your Son."
>
> At 4 p.m. the US Army, the CIA and the FBI visited the house of the old man, took the whole garden apart, searched every inch, but couldn't find anything. Disappointed they left the house.
>
> A day later the old man received another email from his son. "Beloved Father, I hope the garden is dug up by now and you can plant your potatoes. That is all I could do for you from here. Love, Your Son."

Here are four situations that need creative problem solving ideas. Choose two of them and with paper and pencil write your ideas.

Creative problem solving

1. Large flocks of starlings have created a public nuisance in many cities. Think up six possible solutions to this problem.

2. A family of chipmunks are boring holes under the porch of your home and are destroying the structure. List 10 ways you can deal with them.

3. You have four children, who have indicated they want to visit you at the same time in your rather small apartment. Although you certainly want to see them all, it'll be overwhelming to have them all come at once. You do not want to offend any of them. What can you do? Think of at least six different solutions.

4. Getting in and out of your car is becoming more difficult as you get older. Think of at least seven creative ideas to solve this difficulty.

29 Imagination

In her weekly column in "Parade Magazine," Marilyn vos Savant helps stimulate imagination in a feature titled "What Would You Say?" For example: "Joseph P. Kennedy said, 'When the going gets tough, the tough get going.' What would you say?" Some responses she received: "When the going gets tough, don't expect much company." "When the going gets tough, marinate!" "When the going gets tough, I go to Grandmas'."

Now stretch your imagination. Pick three of the following and write your answer to each of them.

Imagination

1. Piney the Elder wrote, "Home is where the heart is." What would you say?

2. An American proverb says, "If it ain't broke, don't fix it." What would you say?

3. Geoffry Chaucer wrote, "People who live in glass houses shouldn't throw stones." What would you say?

4. Fanny Fern wrote, "The way to a man's heart is through his stomach." What would you say?

5. An English proverb says, "Actions speak louder than words." What would you say?

30 Tall tales

The Burlington Liar's Club of Burlington, Wisconsin, has an annual contest to see who can think up the biggest lie or tall tale. Here are several examples:

- The lake was so small the fish were curved.
- It rained so hard the water was backed up against a barbed wire fence.
- The mosquitoes were so smart a camper woke up to find four of them using a firefly to burn a hole in the netting of her tent.

Now it's your turn. Try to generate at least three tall tales, the taller the better, and share them with a friend or family member.

31 **What if**

Here's another chance to enhance your powers of imagination. Write at least three consequences of each of the following propositions.

What if

1. What if people could fly like birds?

2. What if cars didn't need people to drive them?

3. What if cats could talk like people?

4. What if ice didn't melt no matter how warm it was?

5. What if a cell phone could read your mind so you didn't have to punch in the number?

6. What if all of your clothes were self-cleaning?

7. What if you had three arms?

32 What's the question?

Write a question for each of the following answers. Be as creative as possible. For example:

1. 8:30 a.m. *What time do you usually leave for work?*

2. No! _____

   _____

3. My back hurts. _____

   _____

4. Yes! _____

   _____

5. A dozen roses _____

   _____

6. I feel grumpy _____

   _____

7. The Chicago White Sox _____

   _____

8. About 70 _____

   _____

9. My rain coat _____

_____

10. Red, white and blue _____

_____

11. No good _____

_____

12. A bowl of soup _____

_____

33 Listing

Writing down your ideas is one of the best ways to stimulate your brain. Your thinking is coordinated with the movement of your hand as you write, which causes more neuron and dendrite activity in your brain.

Choose two of the following and write your answers.

Listing

1. List at least 15 uses your grandmother made of her large apron.

2. List all of the things you can think of that are sticky. Select 20 of your best ideas.

3. List 25 things that can be used as containers.

4. You have just completed the training at the Baskin-Robbins Ice Cream School. For your final test, you must make and name an entirely new ice cream. List 8 suggestions.

5. You have just opened a hotdog restaurant. What are 15 different ways you can serve a hot dog?

6. How has flying in an airplane changed your life? List at least 12 ways.

34 What kind of older person are you?

Using the following questions as a guide, write a description of yourself as an older person.

What kind of older person are you?

1. Describe your physical self.

2. Where do you live?

3. What clothes do you wear?

4. What colors do you like?

5. Describe your health.

6. What are major challenges in your life?

7. What are your dreams?

Now here's a bigger challenge for your brain. Using your pencil, draw a picture of yourself. Use simple lines and shapes—nothing fancy. Stick figures are fine. If you have crayons or colored pencils, add color to your drawing. Sketch a picture of where you live.

The next step is to imagine you could transform yourself into a different older person. Using the seven questions above, describe this older person. Then change your drawings to conform to your new self.

35 Two cartoons

Have you ever wondered how people who draw cartoons come up with such clever words? Here's your chance to use your imagination.

What is the woman saying to the dog as she runs from the bathtub? Write down four possibilities.

1. _____

   _____

2. _____

   _____

3. _____

   _____

4. _____

   _____

What are the men saying as they gaze at the flower?
Think of four possibilities.

1. _____
   _____

2. _____
   _____

3. _____
   _____

4. _____
   _____

36 Be a composer

Think of a tune you know well and write new words to it. For example:

> Are you sleeping, are you sleeping, brother John, brother John? Morning bells are ringing, morning bells are ringing, ding, ding, dong, ding, ding, dong.

New words could be:

> Are you hungry, are you hungry, sister Kay, sister Kay? Dinner bells are gonging, dinner bells are gonging, gong, gong, ging, gong, gong, ging. *[It's okay to make up new words.]*

Try new words to this one:

> I've been working on the railroad all the live-long day. I've been working on the railroad just to pass the time of day. Can't you hear the whistle blowin', rise up so early in the morn.

This exercise challenges your creativity. Let your mind spin off and see what comes out. It doesn't have to make good sense.

37 Bumper stickers

People display bumper stickers to express their thoughts and feelings about everything from pets to politics. For example, you've probably seen stickers similar to these:

- I'D RATHER BE SKIING
- HONK IF YOU LIKE GARDENING

Select four from the following list and create a custom bumper sticker for each of them. Write them down so you can share them with others.

Bumper Stickers

1. A favorite football or baseball player
2. A grandmother
3. A gardener
4. A birder
5. Peace
6. Your hometown
7. Your favorite restaurant
8. A lover of cars

38 What in the world do you know?

Write the answers to the questions below about each picture. (See Appendix A for answers.)

1. Is this structure more than 300 years old? _____

2. In what country is it located? _____

3. Is the country larger than Mexico? _____

4. Is this place north or south of the equator? _____

5. On what continent is it located? _____

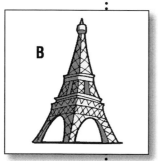

1. Is this structure more than 300 years old? _____

2. In what country is it located? _____

3. Is the country larger than Mexico? _____

4. Is this place north or south of the equator? _____

5. On what continent is it located? _____

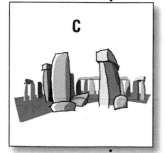

1. Is this structure more than 300 years old? _____

2. In what country is it located? _____

3. Is the country larger than Mexico? _____

4. Is this place north or south of the equator? _____

5. On what continent is it located? _____

1. Is this structure more than 300 years old? _____

2. In what country is it located? _____

3. Is the country larger than Mexico? _____

4. Is this place north or south of the equator? _____

5. On what continent is it located? _____

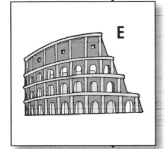

1. Is this structure more than 300 years old? _____

2. In what country is it located? _____

3. Is the country larger than Mexico? _____

4. Is this place north or south of the equator? _____

5. On what continent is it located? _____

39 Things that ping

Fluency is the ability to think of many answers to a question or to list many possible solutions to a problem. Check your fluency by listing as many things as you can that ping. For example:

- A bad car engine
- A guitar string
- Hail hitting a metal roof

On a separate piece of paper see if you can list at least 10 more things that ping.

40 Time out

Suppose all of the clocks in the world stopped running or disappeared for a month. What other methods might be used for measuring the passage of time? For example:

- Burn a candle of a certain size.
- Measure the length of shadows.
- Chart the movement of the stars.

See if you can list at least seven more ways to chart time.

41 Design a door

Choose four of the following places: Your bedroom, a hair salon, a doctor's office, a mansion, a bakery, a humane society for animals, a hardware store, an artist's studio. Draw the outline of four doors on a piece of paper or use the blank doors that follow. Write the name of the places you've chosen under each one. Now decorate a door that would be especially appropriate for each of these places.

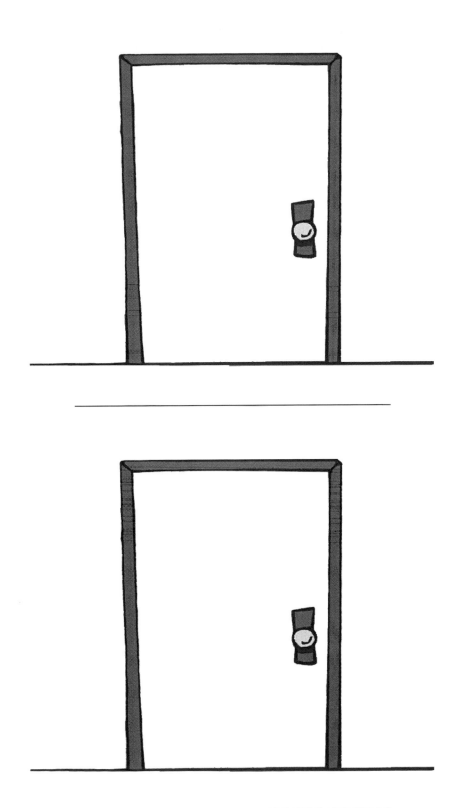

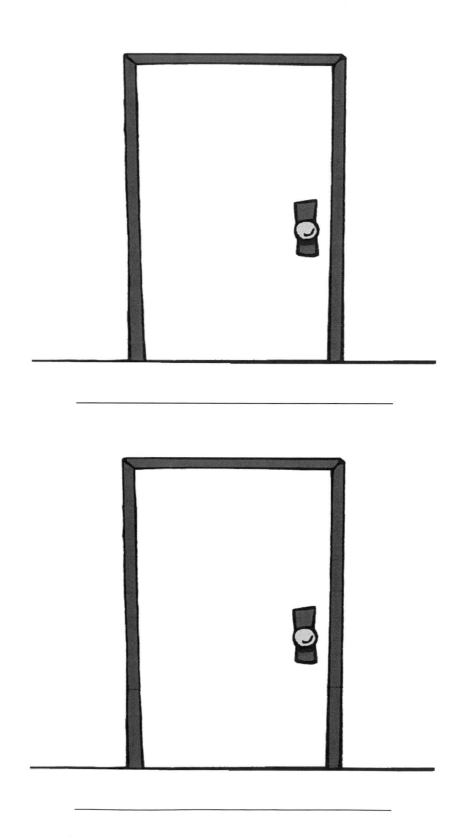

SIX

words, words, words

We're verbal creatures whose brains thrive on words. If we didn't have words, how would we communicate? Perhaps by sign language or other body motions, but for most of us words are basic to our everyday life. There are hundreds of ways to challenge our brains using words.

Think of all the things we do with words. The first thing we acquire when we enter this world is a name, an identity we carry with us all our lives. We use endless metaphors such as "He's two sandwiches short of a picnic" and "She's a few cookies short of a dozen," or figures of speech such as "couch potato," "strange bedfellows," "cream of the crop," "a wolf in sheep's clothing" and "steal someone's thunder." And then there's fowl language. Best not to go there!

A good basic exercise with words is to make a habit of looking up one new word a day. You may know the meaning of the word, but see what the dictionary has to say. As you read the newspaper or magazines or listen to the TV, be sure to look up words that are new to you. This is an easy way to build your vocabulary, create new brain circuits AND have fun.

42 The end's the same

Each of the following groups takes the same three-letter word to complete all the words in the group. Complete each group and then check Appendix A for the answers.

1. Mot __ __ __   4. Sen __ __ __

   Wit __ __ __   Deb __ __ __

   Bot __ __ __   Rot __ __ __

   Hit __ __ __   Pir __ __ __

2. Sav __ __ __   5. Fri __ __ __

   Gar __ __ __   Leg __ __ __

   Voy __ __ __   Off __ __ __

   Man __ __ __   Def __ __ __

3. Don __ __ __   6. Lis __ __ __

   Tur __ __ __   Kit __ __ __

   Hoc __ __ __   Mit __ __ __

   Mon __ __ __   Has __ __ __

43   **Word quadruplets**

Add a letter to each word below so that you can form four new words by rearranging the four letters. For example: add M to TIE and get TIME, MITE, EMIT, ITEM.

1. Tie _____ _____ _____ _____

2. Mat _____ _____ _____ _____

3. Top _____ _____ _____ _____

4. Sea _____ _____ _____ _____

5. Lea _____ _____ _____ _____

6. Ail _____ _____ _____ _____

7. Men _____ _____ _____ _____

8. Ore _____ _____ _____ _____

9. Lie _____ _____ _____ _____

10. Ted _____ _____ _____ _____

44   Kitchen quiz

These scrambled words are articles found in most kitchens. Unscramble the letters and write the word in the blank. (See Appendix A for answers.)

1. painkns   _____

2. rofk   _____

3. sanpscue   _____

4. psono   _____

5. tellisk   _____

6. chlothisd   _____

7. koclc   _____

8. kleteatte   _____

9. treosat   _____

10. salpte   _____

45   Spoonerisms

In the late 1800s a scholar and well-respected author in Oxford, England, Reverend William Archibald Spooner, slipped up when announcing the name of a hymn. He meant to say, "Conquering Kings Their Titles Take." But what came out was "Kinquering Kongs Their Titles Take" We're told the audience of Oxford students held their laughter but then began inventing more topsy-turvy expressions. Spooner was a good sport and went along with the joke, contributing many goofs of his own. By 1900 the word "spoonerisms" had entered the language.

When Spooner died in 1930, his obituary ran for a full column, most of it examples of his fractured language. The following are some of his best:

- It's kistomary to cuss the bride.
- A blushing crow.
- I was hocked and shorrified.
- He joins this club over my bed toddy.
- He rode off on his well-boiled icicle.

Now try devising some of your own spoonerisms. As a beginning see what you can do with these song titles: "Red Sails in the Sunset," "Don't Fence Me In," "When Johnny Comes Marching Home."

46 Words have this in common

1. What do the following words have in common? (See Appendix A for answer.)

brag	golf	flow	keep
live	mood	pools	emit
snap	part	gulp	dial
reward	deliver	strap	sleek

2. What do these 10 words have in common? (See Appendix A for answer.)

art	must	let	turn	pot
asp	be	on	ok	rut

47 Vanity license plates

People have a different kind of logic from that of computers. It's called "fuzzy logic." We can make sense of things even without complete information. We add data from our own experiences. For example: What do you make of this license plate: ZPNALNG? It probably means "Zipping along." How about these?

ALELU1A   XILDTXN   S CAPE   NDAMOOD

Now try to develop some other vanity tags, keeping in mind that you can use only seven letters or less. You'll marvel at your mental agility.

48 Letter writing

One researcher says that an excellent brain stretcher is to write for half an hour every day. Does that seem like a lot? Perhaps. But how about writing a letter to someone at least once a week? Your letter could become the highlight of someone else's day. Also, sharing your thoughts makes you feel great.

49 Run-on words

The challenge is to find the way these letters can go together to make sense. For example: He re com est hera in (Here comes the rain.)

1. Ho meo nth era nge.

2. IR SJF KFB IC IA

3. Ro sesa re re dvi olets ar ebl ue.

4. Ipl ed geal le gian cet oth efl ag.

5. B epa tien twi tha llth atisun answe rediny ourh ear tandt ryto lo veth equest ions.

(See Appendix A for answers.)

50 Word pairs

The English language has a tendency to pair words. For instance: Black and white, salt and pepper. After each word listed, write another word that's often used with it.

1. Paper or _____

2. Soup or _____

3. Left or _____

4. This or _____

5. Smoking or _____

6. Sink or _____

7. Up or _____

8. Sweet or _____

9. Rent or _____

10. Half empty or _____

11. Life or _____

12. Love 'em or _____

13. Pen or _____

14. Good or _____

15. Better or _____

16. Whole wheat or _____

17. Sooner or _____

18. Hot or _____

19. Red or _____

20. Now or _____

51   More word pairs

1. Chips and _____

2. Ebb and _____

3. Eat and _____

4. Ken and _____

5. Sick and _____

6. Wine and _____

7. Mix and _____

8. Alive and _____

9. Bed and _____

10. Rice and _____

11. Walk and _____

12. Cut and _____

13. Jekyll and _____

14. Kiss and _____

15 Wash and _____

16. Inhale and _____

17. Nuts and _____

18. Shoes and _____

19. Meat and _____

20. Sweet and _____

52 Haiku

Haiku is Japanese verse set in three unrhymed lines of 5, 7 and 5 syllables, for a total of 17 syllables. Originally the verses referred to the season, but the artform has now evolved to include anything going on in the poet's life. Now imagine you're the poet and write a Haiku about the weather, an old tree, a flower garden, how you're feeling and so forth. Here are two examples:

Morning fog sinking
Creates a silver blanket
For the sleeping earth.

Moon high in the sky
Tipped as an empty bowl
No spills until morn.

It may sound difficult, but in fact it's quite easy. We're all poets at heart. Remember that doing something new and different is excellent exercise for the brain. Try it—you'll like it!

53 The paomnnehal pweor of the hmuan mind

Aoccdring to a rscheearch at Cmabrigde Uinervtisy, it deosn't mattaer in what order the ltteers in a word are, the only ipromatnt thing is that the frist and lsat ltteer be in the rghit pclae.The rset can be a taotl mses and you can still raed it wouthit a porbelm. This is bcuseae the human mind deos not raed ervy lteter by istlef, but the word as a wlohe.

Amazing isn't it? Who ever said you had to spell correctly?

54 Rebuses

Rebuses are visual or verbal puzzles that present in pictorial form a word or a familiar phrase. Much can be deduced from a word's position. For example, the word "once" is presented above the word "lightly," so the answer is "once over lightly." If the letters "g-o-s-s-i-p" are arranged vertically, or in a column, the answer is "gossip column."

Here are some rebuses that will wipe the cobwebs from your brain. (See Appendix A for answers.)

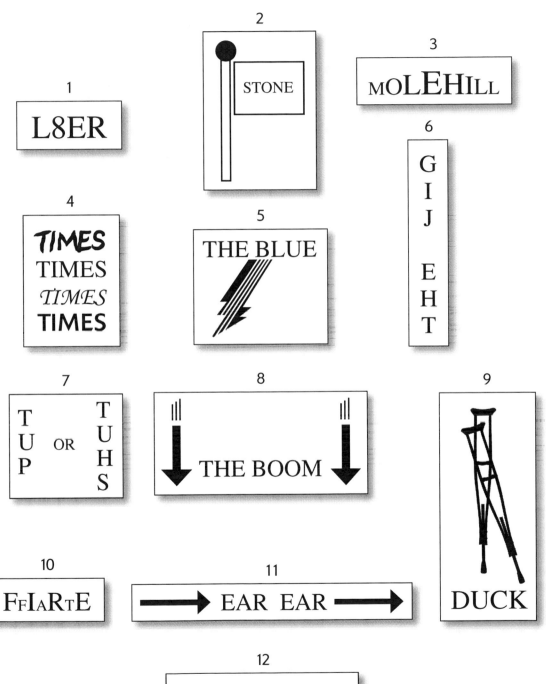

1

L8ER

2

STONE

3

mOLEHIll

6

G
I
J

E
H
T

4

TIMES
TIMES
TIMES
TIMES

5

THE BLUE

7

T   T
U   U
  OR   H
P   S

8

THE BOOM

9

DUCK

10

FFIARTE

11

EAR EAR

12

Invent one of your own.

55 More rebuses

(See Appendix A for answers.)

1

PEANUST
ALMONSD PECNAS

2

BLIND
THE BLIND
THE BLIND
THE BLIND

3

R
E
A
D
I
N
G

4

EGG
HISFACE

5

THRfrogOAT

6

CALLED CALLED CALLED
CALLED CALLED CALLED
CALLED CALLED CALLED
CALLED CALLED CALLED

CHOSEN CHOSEN CHOSEN

7

D A N C E
A   C
N   N
C   A
E C N A D

8

     RAIN
CALM SNOW
     HAIL

9

OPEN &

BOARD

10

    H
    A
WIN N
    D
    S

11

RALLY RALLY RALLY
RALLY FLAG RALLY
RALLY RALLY RALLY

12

Invent one of your own.

56 Palindromes

Palindromes are words, phrases or sentences that read the same forward or backward. Write a palindrome that relates to each word or phrase below. For example: A small dog (pup); a girl's name (Anna).

1. A female sheep __ __ __
2. Something that doesn't work __ __ __
3. Another word for night __ __ __
4. Cheerleaders have it __ __ __
5. A way to form a kind of lace __ __ __
6. Necessary to see __ __ __
7. Twelve o'clock in midday __ __ __ __
8. A tool used by builders __ __ __ __
9. Songs sung alone __ __ __ __ __
10. A boat similar to a canoe __ __ __ __ __ __
11. A car used in racing __ __ __ __ __ __ __
12. A bone found in a bird __ __ __ __ __ __ __ __

(See Appendix A for answers.)

Now think up some of your own palindromes. Start with three letters and see if you can work up to five or more letters. Feel your dendrites grow!

If you like this exercise and are familiar with the Internet, do a search using the word *palindrome* and be surprised at others who have found palindromes mind stretching.

57   Wildflowers we love

In this jumble of letters you'll find all the words listed on the next page. The words can read across, up, down, or diagonally. It's a good brain builder to do these kinds of puzzles. (See Appendix A for answers.)

```
                        J
                    D   A   S
                O   T   C   X   U
            R   E   W   K   L   I   N
        N   L   C   D   I   R   I   S   F
        E   O   O   A   A   N   G   T   H   Z   L
    D   I   W   B   L   I   T   A   S   T   E   R   O
L   V   S   I   C   S   S   H   C   E   P   M   B   R   W
O   B   L   A   C   K   E   Y   E   D   S   U   S   A   N   L   E
G   X   I   H   W   H   T   N   Z   P   D   O   C   W   Y   M   I   K   R
P   D   X   J   I   H   N   I   U   A   R   R   E   V   O   L   C
O   B   R   C   I   A   V   L   N   M   E   I   Z   F   O
    P   L   O   S   N   L   P   D   I   T   A   O   L
        P   R   T   E   A   I   E   R   T   R   U
            Y   L   E   U   T   L   P   U   M
                E   U   R   Z   I   Y   B
                    Q   E   W   O   I
                        L   P   N
                            E
```

ASTER	IRIS
BLACK-EYED SUSAN	JACK-IN-THE-PULPIT
BUTTERCUP	LAUREL
CHICORY	LILY
CLOVER	POPPY
COLUMBINE	PRIMROSE
COWSLIP	QUEEN ANNE'S LACE
DAISY	SUNFLOWER
DANDELION	THISTLE
GOLDENROD	VIOLET

58 Word search

The letters below are all mixed up, but hidden among them are words that describe things you can do with your brain.

The words can be read across, up, down or diagonally. If you can locate all 12 words you're really using your brain. (See Appendix A for answers.)

Q	A	S	B	R	E	A	D	C	D
T	E	E	X	L	Z	O	P	N	R
H	I	E	W	H	S	B	A	P	K
I	E	A	B	C	O	T	D	E	N
N	F	A	D	G	S	P	I	J	O
K	K	L	R	R	M	N	E	T	W
O	G	U	E	S	S	P	Q	A	R
S	T	D	A	U	F	E	E	L	V
W	N	X	M	Y	Z	A	B	K	C
U	D	B	E	L	I	E	V	E	F

SEE	TALK	GUESS
HEAR	HOPE	DREAM
READ	KNOW	BELIEVE
FEEL	THINK	UNDERSTAND

59 Crossword puzzles

People often ask, "Is doing crossword puzzles good stimulation for the brain?" The answer is a big YES! Furthermore, publishers have caught on that crossword puzzles support brain fitness and are big business.

Check the games section of most bookstores and you'll find row after row of crossword puzzle books. *The New York Times* has published an entire series of books including *Fitness for the Mind Crosswords.* AARP has jumped on the bandwagon with titles such as *Awesome Crosswords to Keep You Sharp, Baffling Crosswords to Keep You Sharp* and *Clever Crosswords to Keep You Sharp.* There are 50 puzzles in each book. There are books of riddle crosswords and twisted crosswords. There are puzzle books with section titles such as Easy Monday, Tougher Tuesday, Harder Wednesday, Killer Thursday and Cranium Crushing Friday. Most of these books are spiralbound so they lay flat. An endless number of dictionaries will help you along the way.

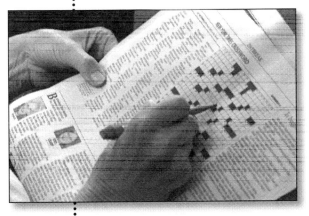

So if you're into crosswords, and especially if you're not, check out the feast at your nearest bookstore. It'll put a smile on your face and a charge to your brain.

60 Magnetic word kits

Consider buying a magnetic word kit of over 240 magnetized words (available at most bookstores). Install them on a fridge, file cabinet, locker door, cookie sheet or any other steel surface and watch the sentences, or poems if you choose, emerge as you arrange them. This tool is good for building creativity, imagination and language. It's fun to pick off a word, put it together with several other words and see what weird combinations come out.

SEVEN

power up your mind with puzzles and numbers

There are people who:

- Enjoy working with numbers and can do mental calculations.
- Can easily balance their checkbook.
- Enjoy games that require logical and statistical thinking such as checkers or chess.
- Identify the logical flaws in things people say and do.
- Found math and science to be their favorite subjects in school.
- Take a systematic approach to problem solving.
- Like to find patterns and relationships between objects or numbers.

Do these characteristics fit you? If so, this chapter will be easy and fun. If not, you may want to be particularly conscientious about doing these exercises. Research has proven that it's possible to improve brain functions by regularly working with numbers and solving puzzles that stimulate your brain.

61   Sudoku

Have you tried the new number game, Sudoku, that is appearing in hundreds of newspapers throughout the United States? It's the latest craze in games. Almost overnight many folks are talking about it and doing it. There's no adding or other math involved. It's a game of logic.

It's believed that Howard Garns, a retired architect from Indianapolis, Indiana, is the puzzle's inventor. He was 74 years old when he sold his first "Number Place" puzzle. He died in 1989, not living long enough to see his puzzle become a success.

An editor of a puzzle magazine in Japan saw one of the puzzles, took it home, changed its name to Sudoku and introduced it in his publications, where it became a hit.

Numbers do tend to scare some of us, but knowing that it's important to do new and different things, give it a try.

Begin with grids rated easy and then proceed to those rated more difficult. In case your newspaper doesn't carry the puzzles, here's a Sudoku rated one star, the easiest.

5		3	8	1	9		2	
8	1		4			3	9	5
	4	2				7	8	1
6		8	3		1		7	
								8
1		9	5	7			4	6
2				8		9	5	3
		5		9	6			
4			7		5	8	6	2

The rules are simple: Complete the grid so that every row, column and 3 x 3 box contains every digit from 1 to 9 inclusively.

If you like this challenge, go to your nearest bookstore, where you'll find dozens of Sudoku books to choose from. If you prefer, go on the web and do a search for "Sudoku." You'll find good information and many more puzzles.

No matter how good or poor you are at Sudoku, you can be sure you'll get a good brain workout, especially in your left brain where abilities with numbers tend to reside.

62 Mahjong

An old game that's popular with some older people is Mahjong. The game is played with tiles similar in function to playing cards. The object is somewhat like that of gin rummy, where players attempt to collect sets and sequences. But in Mahjong, the values of winning hands can vary wildly. The game is played by four people, but not partners. The object of the game is to score the most points, which are earned for "going Mahjong," and for holding certain combinations of tiles.

Although descended from ancient Chinese games, Mahjong in its current form is only about 100 years old. There are several main systems of rules, but the most common in the United States is the American system.

Why learn to play? Instead of playing the same game or games over and over, which is not much of a challenge for our brains, this might be just the ticket to spark those synapses.

63 Go figure

I. An appliance retailer purchased a dishwasher at a wholesale price of $885 and priced it for sale in his store at a retail price of 18% above the wholesale price. During a special promotion, he discounted the retail price by 10%. What was the special promotion price of the dishwasher?

2. Chickens are $.50 cents each, ducks are $3 each and turkeys are $10 each. You want to spend exactly $100, but also take home 100 birds. How many of each bird should you buy? (See Appendix A for answers.)

64 Addition and subtraction

Place + and − signs between the digits so that both sides of the equation are equal.

For example: 3 + 2 + 1 - 4 + 1 + 3 = 6

Now try these:

4	9	3	7	3	1	= 19
9	8	6	3	5	1	= 6
3	5	3	9	6	5	= 13

(See Appendix A for answers.)

Go another step and invent some of your own addition and subtraction problems, following this format.

What number should take the place of the question mark?

5	6	7	8	9	?	____
61	52	63	94	46	?	____

(See Appendix A for answers.)

65 Mental agility

Match the line patterns in the top row with each pattern in the lower rows. Put the corresponding number in each empty box. Take your time. Be aware of stretching your mind.

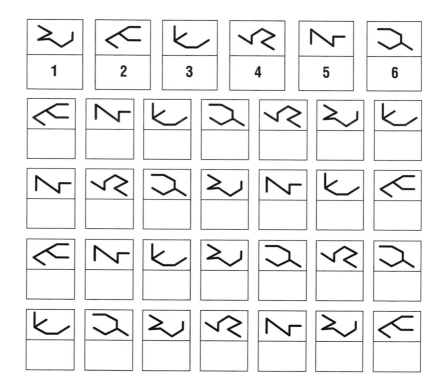

(See Appendix A for answers.)

66 Toothpick puzzle

Here's a toothpick puzzle invented by Martin Gardner of Norma, Oklahoma, who is 90 years old.

Arrange nine toothpicks to form 100. Now alter the position of only two toothpicks to spell the word CAT. (Tip: Turn the toothpicks in several directions to see new possibilities.)

(See Appendix A for answer.)

67 Walking toothpicks

While you have the toothpicks at hand, try doing this puzzle. Arrange the toothpicks as shown below. By moving only five toothpicks, make three squares that are exactly the same.

(See Appendix A for answer.)

68 Tangram fun

A tangram set is a square that's been divided into seven simple shapes called "tans." These include two large triangles, two smaller triangles, a medium triangle, a square and a parallelogram. When moved about, these shapes can convey the ideas, thoughts and emotions of the player. Or they can be just plain fun.

Tangrams is an ancient Chinese game whose origins are lost in history. One unlikely theory is that a tile maker named Tan accidentally invented the game when he dropped a tile that broke into the seven shapes.

Tangrams became very popular in the United States, Asia, and Europe in the 1800s. The game was played by young and old, male and female, rich and poor. Famous people such as Edgar Allan Poe, Napoleon and John Quincy Adams were known to enjoy the game.

Playing tangrams can be as simple or as difficult as you want to make it. Using a blank piece of paper, trace the figure on the next page. Cut out the seven pieces. For your first puzzle put the seven tans back into a square. Try not to peek at the original diagram.

Now try to form some shapes: Cat, dog, cow, woman, man, rooster, house, barn.

The idea is to use all the pieces to create a shape. All pieces must touch, lying flat with no overlapping. Usually the shape to be made is in the form of a silhouette. The possibilities are endless. Have fun!

(See Appendix A for ideas of shapes to create.)

Tangram Square

strengthen your sense of smell and taste

Have you ever thought about the fact that the information entering your brain comes in through the five senses: Sight, hearing, smell, taste and touch? We usually take these abilities for granted, but as we age it's important to maintain and strengthen these senses.

Smell is probably the sense we most underestimate. Of all our senses, smell is the most basic. We're told that smell was the first of our senses, and it was so successful that in time the small lump of olfactory tissue atop the nerve cord grew into a brain. We think because we smelled!

69 Aromas

Some of our strongest memories relate to aromas. Maya Angelo remembers that her grandmother would parboil an orange, stick cloves into the peel, wrap it up and then a week before Christmas unwrap it so the pungent aroma of oranges and cloves permeated the whole house.

If possible make an orange with cloves. It would be a big plus for your sense of smell. And it doesn't have to be Christmas.

70 Bring the scents of nature inside

In her *Grow Dendrites Forever* workbook, Cindy Short suggests that to enhance your sense of smell, bring the scents of nature inside: Add plants, flowers, potpourri and herbs to your environment. (Do you know about scented geraniums?)

She also suggests that in your ventures in the kitchen you try using spices with strong smells such as curry, lemon, cinnamon and, of course, cilantro.

71 A sensory bath

Plan a sensory bath. Draw a tub of warm water, add bubble bath or aromatic salts or oils. Include a sponge or loofah or body scrub. Add candlelight, music and a soft towel and you're ready for a relaxing time.

You may be saying, that's too much trouble. Not really. Your brain likes it when you're good to yourself.

When you smell the aromas of your bath again or hear the music, you'll remember to relax and be calm.

72 Surround yourself with your favorite aromas

As a way to enhance your sense of smell, purchase a scented candle or some potpourri. We're told lavender is especially relaxing and mint is a natural brain stimulant. You may want to visit a cosmetic counter and ask to smell different soaps and perfumes. It's free, you know.

Don't forget incense. Our generation associated incense with hippies and other off-beat types, but why should they have all the sensory stimulation? Go ahead, try some incense!

73 Hold your nose

Lawrence Katz, in his book *Keep Your Brain Alive,* says that most of what we call taste actually depends on smell. He advocates holding your nose as you try different foods to note how smell and taste work together. If you can't smell it, how does it taste?

Katz also suggests that to change your usual morning olfactory association (wake up and smell the coffee), wake up to something different—vanilla, citrus, peppermint. To do this you could keep an extract of your favorite aroma in an airtight container on your bedside table for a week and release it when you first awaken. What would this do for you? By consistently linking a new odor with your morning routine, you're activating new neural pathways in the brain.

74 Tastebuds

The tastebuds can distinguish four main types of flavors: Sweet, salty, sour and bitter. (See map of tongue on next page.) Some researchers add others such as astringent and metallic.

In the *Brain Workout*, Arthur and Ruth Winter suggest this exercise: Take five envelopes and five cotton swabs and dip one swab in salt, another in lemon, another in sugar,

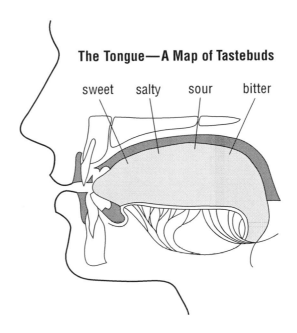

The Tongue—A Map of Tastebuds

sweet   salty   sour   bitter

another in vinegar and the last in water. Then place the swabs in the envelopes with their identifications written on small pieces of paper. Close your eyes.

With one hand, gently touch the top of your tongue with a swab and try to identify the taste. Repeat with the left rear side of your tongue and the right rear side. Write down what you believe the taste is. Wait sixty seconds and repeat with another swab. Repeat the tasting procedure for each swab. Check your answers against the slips of paper in the envelopes.

This could be a fun exercise to do with a friend or perhaps a grandchild.

75 Food and memories

Think of foods that bring back memories of your childhood:

- Cake and ice cream at a birthday party
- S'mores around a bonfire at camp
- Hotdogs at a baseball game

Write down 8–10 memories you associate with specific foods. Don't forget foods you associate with holidays such as Thanksgiving, Christmas and the Fourth of July.

76 Explore new tastes

When you go to the grocery store do you see fruits and vegetables you've never tasted? How about star fruit, pomegranates, mangoes? In the vegetable category, have you tried plantain or some of the hot peppers?

Be brave and buy a new fruit or vegetable and have a tasting time. Your might be surprised at what you like.

How about trying a new kind of cheese? There are dozens of new flavors these days. Or maybe some new cookies.

The idea is to taste something new and different as a way to surprise your tastebuds, which are connected to brain cells.

NINE

have fun with visual arts and illusions

When most of us older adults were growing up, we were expected to follow exactly the directions given to us by our teacher. We were taught to copy, to trace and to be sure to color inside the lines. Being creative in our artwork was not a part of our experience. As a result, many of us struggle to overcome the restrictions and prohibitions we absorbed in those early days. The idea of having the freedom to express our unique ideas using paper, canvas, textiles, clay or other media tends to elude us.

These exercises are designed to loosen up the noodle and give you a fun time with the visual arts.

A hot day in the field

This family picture taken at threshing time about 100 years ago in central Illinois provides an opportunity to focus in detail on the people, clothing, environment and feeling of that moment in time.

Here are some questions that will help you REALLY see:

1. How many people are in the picture?
2. How many men do you see?
3. How many women and children?
4. What ways are they using to protect themselves from the hot sun?
5. Describe the clothing worn by the men and by the women.
6. What is the dark area behind the two standing men?
7. What shapes can you find in the picture?
8. Think about what textures are evident.
9. What is the occasion of these people being together?
10. What is the mood or feeling of the picture?
11. What thoughts come to mind as you look at the picture? Does it bring back any memories?

Using paper and pencil write a paragraph about the picture. You might write it from the standpoint of one person in the photo. You may become aware that you're studying the picture in ways you don't usually do. The more time you spend really seeing a picture, the more you'll appreciate it and the more stimulation it'll provide for the brain.

78 Picnic Time on the Farm

The people in the photograph below are gathered playing some kind of game.

As a way of REALLY seeing, try to answer these questions:

- How many people do you see in this picture?
- How old do you think these people are?
- What time of the year is it?
- What shapes can you find in the picture?
- Any hints as to what the people might have been eating?
- Do you think these people are related to each other?
- What is the occasion for them being together?
- What do you think these people are doing?
- What is the mood or feeling of the picture?
- Does the picture bring back any memories for you?

With paper and pencil write a short story about the picture. Be as creative as you can. Let your imagination run wild and have fun.

79 Palming your eyes

Find a quiet place to sit at a table or desk, putting your elbows on the table. (It's okay, Mom, we're not eating.) Take off your glasses. Rub your palms together vigorously for 20 seconds. Then cup your palms and place them over your closed eyes.

Breathe deeply and rest with your eyes closed for four to five minutes. Then gently open your eyes and notice that everything seems sharper and colors seem brighter.

Try doing this once or twice a day to rest your eyes and to relax.

80 Change of focus

Look at something close to you such as your hand. Then change your focus to the far horizon. Choose a specific place on the horizon and focus on it for several seconds; then come back to your hand. Now look out again and dwell on another element on the far horizon.

This exercise can be practiced a number of times a day and will enliven your eyes and sharpen your perceptions.

81 Widening your vision

Place your index fingers together at eye level, 10–12 inches from your face. Looking ahead, move your fingers slowly away from each other on the horizontal plane. Stop moving your fingers out when you can no longer see them. Then bring your fingers back together and do the same exercise on the vertical plane.

Now relax and think about how this exercise affects your mind and body.

82 Draw an egg

Your first reaction may be that you cannot draw a straight line. Most of us have more artistic ability than we recognize.

Drawing an egg is an excellent way to sharpen your ability to really see.

Set an egg on the table in front of you and find a piece of paper and a pencil. Observe the egg carefully. Then start sketching. The purpose of this exercise is not to see how well you can duplicate the image of an egg, but to sharpen your ability to REALLY SEE. Try sketching what you see several times. Continue to look at the egg. In many ways it's an elusive shape and not easy to draw. Remember that the cells in your brain are dancing because of your efforts.

83 A collage of your life

Using a variety of magazines, newspapers, brochures and advertisements, cut out pictures and make a collage of your life.

Let your imagination run rampant. Don't fret if you can't find just the right picture. You may want to sketch some images that aren't available. Think about using stick figures. Crayons or magic markers might enhance some images.

When you've finished, interpret your collage to anyone who'll pay attention.

84 Circles and squares

Using the circles below, see how many objects or pictures you can make. The circles should be the main part of whatever you make. Using pencil or crayon, add lines to the circles to complete your picture. Try to think of things no one else would think of. Add a title below each object.

Using the squares below, see how many objects or pictures you can make. The square should be the main part of whatever you make. Using pencil or crayon, add lines to the squares to complete your picture. Try to think of things no one else would think of. Add a title below each object.

The circles and squares exercises are simple, yet encourage your brain to be creative. These endeavors tend to stimulate the right side of the brain.

85 Draw a pig

Here's a fun exercise with some interpretation about the kind of person you are.

Using an 8½ x 11 inch piece of paper, draw a pig. You may use pencil, pen, crayons or whatever is at hand. There are no specific directions. Just draw a pig.

(For an interpretation of the drawing, see Appendix A.)

86 Let your artistic abilities shine

Here are some ideas to stimulate your artistic juices:

- Bake a cake and decorate it in some unique way with frosting or flowers or mirrors or small figures. Remember that there has never been and never will be another cake like it.

- Most older men wear a small collection of neckties over and over again, food spots and all. Design a new necktie that would let the world know that the man who wears it is keeping up with the times.

- With paper and pencil design an underground house. Sketch a floor plan and indicate the appearance of the outside, with some landscaping as well.

Choose one of these ideas for a challenging brain workout.

Illusions

Visual illusion such as the ones here are a fun way to stimulate the neurons and dendrites in your brain and to grow new connections. First you see the figure one way; then as you continue to look you see it another way.

1. Old woman or young girl?

Hint: The old woman's nose is the young girl's chin.

2. Woman or clown?

Hint: Try turning the image in different directions.

3. Face of a Native American or an Eskimo?

4. Man playing horn or woman's silhouette?

Hint: The woman's eye is the black speck in front of the mouthpiece of the horn.

If you enjoy looking at illusions, look for the book *Can You Believe Your Eyes?* by J. Richard Block and Harold Yuker. It's a gem!

TEN

build your spatial abilities

Persons who want to be cab drivers in London are required to undergo extensive training. They must learn the names of all the streets and how to drive from one place to another. If you've ever been to London or seen a map of the city, you can imagine that a super effort would be required to develop this spatial ability.

Several years ago a research project was designed to ascertain what was happening in the parts of the brain where spatial abilities reside, usually the left brain. Brain imaging studies revealed that the cabbies who had qualified to drive had a greatly enlarged section of their brain—more neurons, more dendrites and more connections.

This is encouraging news for those of us who have noticed that as we get older our ability to drive or walk to a given place is not as sharp as it used to be. We have to think a little more about directions. Building our spatial abilities is important to maintaining independence. We want to be able to navigate on our own.

These exercises are designed to sharpen your spatial abilities.

88 Jigsaw puzzles

There's probably no better way to exercise the spatial part of your brain than to work jigsaw puzzles. Fitting these little pieces together helps strengthen the part of the brain that controls spatial relations—the ability to recognize how things piece together and how to get from one place to another.

You may have jigsaw puzzles tucked away in a closet or attic. If not, visit a secondhand store and find slightly used puzzles for pocket change. Set them up on a table

near your living center and fit in a few pieces every day. Warning: Puzzles can become quite addictive, especially as you near the finish.

If you feel at home with computers, you'll find jigsaw puzzles available at the click of the mouse.

89 Making your own puzzle

Find an advertisement or a picture in a magazine, something that has both a picture and print. Cut it into pieces at random, scatter the pieces over a table and reassemble them, guided by the visuals and the words.

Begin with a few pieces; then graduate to more pieces. If you have discarded photos, especially ones with people, these can be fun.

If you feel daring, put the pieces together in a crazy, off-beat way and see what images you can create.

90 Planning a route

Draw a map of how to get to a place where you haven't gone recently. Visualize the route and then sketch it on a piece of paper.

When you have gone somewhere, draw a map of where you were after you get home. Whether you walk, ride a bus or drive, this is a valuable exercise. (Probably not so helpful if you fly.)

91 Tile designs

This exercise helps train your visual and spatial logic. Find which of the four designs in the top row have a match among the designs in the bottom row. The designs may be rotated.

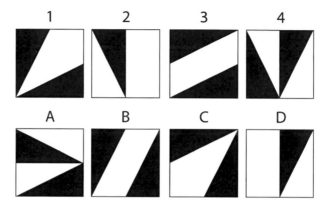

(See Appendix A for answers.)

92 Fun with diagrams and figures

The following three exercises are adapted from material on a cereal box. The original concepts came from Mensa, the high IQ society. Follow the directions for each one.

One of the figures below lacks a common characteristic that the other five figures have. Which one is it and why?

1

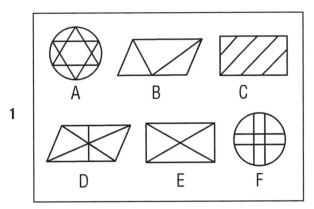

Four of the figures below share a characteristic that the fifth figure doesn't have. Can you determine which figure doesn't go with the others and why?

2

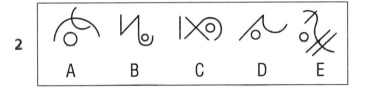

Which of the lower boxes best completes the series on the top?

3

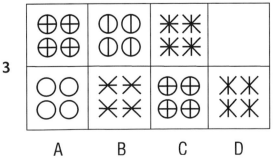

(See Appendix A for answers.)

93   Pencils and more pencils

To sharpen your visual spatial ability observe these pencils for a minute or more. Then write down how many different lengths there are and how many pencils there are of each length.

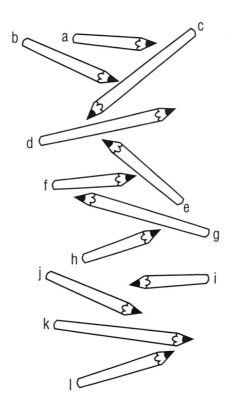

(See Appendix A for answers.)

94 Bottle caps

Compare these two pictures of bottle caps. Which cap in the second picture is not in the first picture?

(See Appendix A for answer.)

95   Name that state

This map of the United States shows the first letter of each state. Write the names of each state starting with the West Coast and moving east.

If you have difficulty with the spelling, consult your dictionary or the spelling tool on your computer.

96   States that end with the letter A

With your list of all the states, count how many end with the letter A. You'll be surprised.

(See Appendix A for answer.)

remember when

Ah, sweet memories. What a lot of pleasure we harvest when we begin to reminisce. Did you know there is an entire body of literature and research studying the value of reminiscing? Sure enough, as we reach the upper edges of our lives, there seem to be mental fitness benefits in recalling and reliving the olden days. There is perhaps one danger—that we live so much in the past that we forget to live in the present.

A basic exercise to sharpen our memories is to let major thoughts of the past sprout additional thoughts. A thought, like a tree, can grow many limbs, branches and leaves. One thought leads to another and before you know it you have evoked a full-grown tree. It's probably best not to say over and over again, "Those were the good 'ole days." Also, it's probably good not to bore your family and friends by repeating memories over and over again.

97 Remember the bath

History reminds us that back in the 1500s baths consisted of a big tub filled with hot water. The man of the house had the privilege of the nice clean water, then all the older sons and men, then the women, and finally the children, the baby last of all. By then the water was so dirty you could actually lose someone in it. Hence the saying, "Don't throw the baby out with the bath water."

Stimulate your memory by recalling how bath time went when you were growing up. How often did you take a bath? Did you have a big tub? How did you heat the water? Who in the family bathed first and who last? What kind of soap did you use? Did everyone have their own towel? What did you do with the dirty bath water? What else do you remember?

98 Bouquets and weddings

In the Middle Ages most people got married in June because they took their yearly bath in May and still smelled pretty good by June. However, they were starting to smell, so brides carried a bouquet of flowers to hide their body odor. Hence we still have the custom today of carrying a bouquet when getting married.

Try to visualize your own wedding or if you didn't marry, a wedding you attended. Where was the wedding held? What did the bride wear? What did the groom wear?

Did she carry flowers? If so, what kind of flowers? Who was invited to the wedding? Was there a party or reception afterward? About how much money was spent on the wedding? Compare the weddings of 50 years ago with today's weddings.

99 Old time cooking

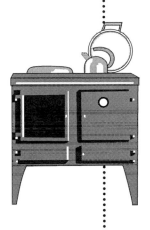

In the old, old days people cooked in the kitchen with a big kettle that always hung over the fire. Every day they lit the fire and added things to the pot. They ate mostly vegetables and not much meat. They would eat the stew for dinner, leaving leftovers in the pot to get cold overnight and then start over the next day. Sometimes stew had food in it that had been there for quite a while. Hence the rhyme, "Peas porridge hot, peas porridge cold, peas porridge in the pot nine days old."

With pencil and paper write down what you ate when you were growing up. Did you have a garden? What did you grow in the garden? Did you preserve the produce in the garden for the winter? How did you do that? When did you eat your meals? Did everyone who lived in your home eat together? Compare what you ate in the past to what you eat now.

100 Memories of pork

In the Middle Ages folks could sometimes obtain pork, which made them feel quite special. When visitors came they would hang their bacon to show it off. "Bringing home the bacon" was a sign of wealth. They would cut off a little to share with guests and then would all sit around and "chew the fat."

Did you have pork to eat? Did you raise the hogs to get the pork? Think about butchering time and all that it entailed. Do you have memories of that activity? Did you hang your bacon or hams? Where did you hang them? There was a saying that folks used everything but the squeal. What did they mean by that?

101 Baking bread

Many years ago bread was divided according to status. Workers got the burnt bottom of the loaf, the family got the middle and guests got the "upper crust."

Was bread baked in your home when you were a child? Recount the steps that went into baking bread. What kinds of breads were made? What kind did you like best? Were special breads made for holidays such as Christmas and Easter? Did you ever think that store-bought bread was better than homemade bread? How do you feel about that now?

102 Down on the farm

Many of us grew up on farms. Tucked away in the back of our minds are memories of those days. Stretching your mind to remember people, animals and activities is good cultivation for the brain.

Speaking of cultivation, what kind of machinery was used on your farm? Were horses still a main source of power? What breed of horses were they? Did you have a tractor? If so, what kind of a tractor was it? Did the tractor make sounds you can remember? What color was it? Do you have any memory of smells associated with the tractor?

When you lived on the farm, who were the neighbors down the road? Did they have children you played with? What kind of games did you play?

What kind of animals did you have on the farm? Did you have a favorite kind of animal? What did you feed the animals? Do you have memories of smells associated with the animals' food? If you had cats and dogs, do you remember their names? Did you have a favorite pet?

Did you raise chickens? Did you purchase baby chicks or did you hatch them? If you hatched them, how did you do that? Recall the sounds of baby chicks and the sounds of the hen and roosters. Can you replicate those sounds? What are your memories of gathering eggs? What was done with all the eggs you gathered? Did you eat some of the chickens? Can you describe how they were prepared for cooking? Did you have a favorite chicken dish?

103 More down on the farm

Did you have a garden on the farm? Describe what you planted and how you planted it. What did you like most about planting and harvesting? What did you like least? Did you have a favorite food from the garden? Describe how it was prepared.

Many farmers had orchards. Did you have an orchard and if so, what kinds of fruit trees did you have? Did you have a grape arbor? What was done with the grapes?

Butchering was a major event on many farms. Did your family butcher? If so, what did they butcher? Describe the activities of butchering day. Do you have memories of the sounds, tastes and smells of this method of providing food for the family?

104 Weather

The weather is important to farmers. How did you get news about the weather? What was the hottest day you remember? What was the coldest day? Did any severe storms leave an impression in your mind? Describe how the sky looked.

Do you remember any times when there were floods? How about draught? What difference did it make to your family if there was too much rain or not enough rain?

Do you have memories of times when you looked at the night sky? Think about scenes of the moon and stars. Did you learn the names of any constellations? What were they? Were you aware of the planets? Name as many as you can. Did you ever see the aurora borealis? Describe the colors and the motion in the sky. Did you ever dream you might someday fly in the sky?

105 Times in your life

Do you remember what you were doing when you were in the first, second and third grades? Describe your classroom or rooms. What were your teachers' names? Do you recall any celebrations of special days? Did you have a favorite subject? a least favorite subject? Recall as many names of your classmates as you can.

What do you remember about high school? What was the building like? Tell how you got to school. How many class sessions were there? Do you recall any special happenings in study halls? What did you do in gym classes? What extracurricular activities did you participate in such as glee club, drama club, student council, school newspaper staff, yearbook staff, basketball, track?

Can you remember any comments your friends wrote in your yearbook? If you danced, what dance steps did you do? Who did you dance with? What was high school graduation like? Describe the music, the speakers, getting your diploma, the parties.

106 Memory and music

Most studies have shown that the right side of the brain is more involved in processing music than the left. This makes sense since the right side is where intuitive, creative and imaginative thinking generally takes place (new studies are not quite so sure). By measuring the blood flow in the brain, researchers have shown that the same areas of the brain that respond with euphoria to stimuli like food, sex and some drugs, also respond to spine-tingling music.

If possible, play a recording of a piece of music that is spine-tingling for you. It would be even better if you could play the music on an instrument. Listen carefully to the

music and recall if you can where you were and what you were doing when you first heard this music. Try to put into words the feelings the music evokes. To clarify your thinking and stimulate your brain even more, take paper and pencil and in a paragraph or two describe the scene, your activity and your feelings.

107 Your first paycheck

What job did you have and how old were you when you received your first paycheck? Do you remember how you felt about earning that money? How did you spend it? List other jobs you had after high school. Name some of the people you worked with.

108 **Remembering**

Here are several exercises to stretch your memory. Pick two and make a list for each.

1. Write down the names of as many kinds of cheese as you can remember. (If you live in Wisconsin, that should be easy.)
2. Write the names of as many kinds of cars as you can recall.
3. List as many kinds of birds as you can.
4. List as many kinds of trees as you can.

(See Appendix A after you've made a good effort.)

109 **How do you want to be remembered?**

Give some thought to how you'd like to be remembered. With paper and pencil, typewriter or computer, write your ideal eulogy. What is it that you've done in your life you'd like family and friends to remember? Try to assess the kind of person you've been and put into words thoughts about your legacy. What do want to live on after you're gone?

You may hesitate to think about this, but it's just the kind of exercise that will stretch your brain and create new connections.

110 Little remembered facts about presidents

Looking at the pictures of 12 Presidents on the next page, match each of the following little known facts with a President.

1. Orphaned at age nine _____

2. Purchased Louisiana from France _____

3. Appointed first woman to the Supreme Court

   _____

4. Established Medicare _____

5. First television campaign _____

6. First Republican President _____

7. First to appoint an African American Secretary of State _____

8. Unanimously elected twice _____

9. Had three different Vice Presidents

   _____

10. Passed anticrime laws _____

11. First graduate of U.S. Naval Academy to become President _____

12. Middle name just the initial "S" because of family disagreement _____

111 Remembering other facts about presidents

Looking at the pictures of the Presidents, write down at least two familiar facts about each of those pictured.

112 Remember Burma Shave?

In 1925 the Burma-Vita Corporation of Minneapolis began producing signs for a campaign that would soon propel the company into the position of number two seller of men's shaving cream.

At the height of their popularity there were 7,000 Burma Shave signs stretching across America. They were a welcome advertising diversion and delightful entertainment for motorists. Even homesick GIs posted Burma Shave signs around the world wherever they went.

Some say the signs were a precursor to modern billboards on American highways. The signs came down in 1963.

Now scratch your head (or your beard) and see if you have a Burma Shave verse tucked in your long-term memory.

Here are a few goodies:

• He lit a match—To check the tank—That's why they call him—Skinless Frank. Burma Shave

• Use our cream—And we betcha—Girls won't wait—They'll come and getcha. Burma Shave

- Henry the 8th—Sure had trouble—Short term wives—Long term stubble. Burma Shave

- Train approaching—Whistle squealing—Pause, avoid that—Run Down Feeling. Burma Shave.

- Her chariot—Raced at eighty per—They hauled away—What had Ben Hur. Burma Shave.

- The whale put Jonah—Down the hatch—But coughed him up—Because he scratched. Burma Shave.

Now fire up your neurons and make up at least one Burma Shave rhyme of your own. Now try for two or more and share with old friends.

If your interest is sparked by this exercise, you might enjoy the book *The Verse by the Side of the Road*. You can also check the website <u>http://seniors-site.com/funstuff/burma.html</u> for more.

113 More Burma Shave rhymes

- Trains don't wander—All over the map—Cause nobody sits—On the Engineer's lap. Burma Shave.

- Don't try passing—On a slope—Unless you have—A periscope. Burma Shave.

- Drinking drivers—Nothing worse—He put the quart—Before the hearse. Burma Shave.

- Grandpa's beard—Was stiff and coarse—And that's what—Caused his fifth divorce. Burma Shave.

- School ahead—Take it slow—Let the little—Shavers grow. Burma Shave.

- Cattle crossing—Means go slow—That old bull—is some cow's beau. Burma Shave.

Try to compose your very own Burma Shave rhyme.

TWELVE

games
make brains

Here's some exciting news about playing games: A 20 year study of over 450 elderly people living in New York showed that reading and playing board games or a musical instrument was associated with a decreased risk of Alzheimer's or other forms of dementia. Participants who worked crossword puzzles four days a week, for instance, had a 47 percent lower risk of dementia than those who did puzzles only once a week.

A number of exercises in this book could be classified as games, but in light of this new insight about game playing, it's important to say more about games and brain stimulation.

Researchers are finding that games and play are important factors in a happy, well-adjusted life. They define play as engaging in activities that are highly gratifying, lack any economic significance, cause no social harm and do not necessarily lead to praise or recognition from others.

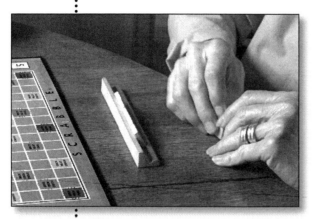

Most games involve our brains in logical activities. Card games such as bridge and pinochle are super mind boosters. Crossword puzzles, chess, cribbage, checkers and Scrabble® are sure to stir up your dendrites.

In all of this game playing, be sure to avoid habit, which is a great enemy of mental acuity. Although playing games is a good thing, always playing the same games stimulates the same cerebral circuits in your brain and leaves other regions unexercised. Take an interest in activities you don't know.

The following workouts are designed to foster a playful attitude and hopefully some laughter.

114 A game party

Invite friends over for a game party. Tell them you're going to play games that you all played as kids. Remember: Hide the thimble; Button, button, who's got the button; I'm going to California and I'm going to take _____" or "When my ship comes in I'll _____"; charades; twenty questions; telegrams; rock, paper, scissors. You probably remember many more. It would be good mental exercise to search the library or a bookstore for books of old-time games to play at your game party. If there's a game store or toy store in your vicinity, make a visit and perhaps purchase a new game or two. Look for Mad Gab. It's great fun and will add zest to your life.

Big Book of Rules by Stephanie Spadaccuic will help you recall board games, kids' games and card games as well as give you all the rules for playing.

115 Hand-eye coordination

Think about activities that require cooperation between your hands and your head, hand-eye coordination. The hand is the primary instrument that carries out the motor commands of the brain. In fact, the hand can be thought of as an extension of the brain. Every waking minute, there's feedback between the hands and the brain. Thus brain performance and hand dexterity are closely connected.

Think of some of the games you played when you were younger. Remember jacks, Tinker Toys, Legos, magic tricks. Try to think of at least three more games that require hand-eye coordination. Now make an effort to find one or more of these games and play them. You'll boost your brain power!

116 Pickup sticks

Look in your closet or attic for the old game of Pick-Up Sticks. Remember it's played with color-coded sticks. The object of the game is to pick up sticks with the highest level of points without disturbing the others. One stray move and you must start over. Keep practicing.

Remember that training the hand in this kind of motor skill is really aimed at enhancing your brain.

117 Dominoes

Various games can be played with dominoes, but this one focuses on hand-eye coordination. Remember how you used to set up the dominoes in a row so if you touched one they all fell down? Try it again and see how many you can set up without a "fall down."

This story is meant as encouragement: "A sparrow knocked over 23,000 dominoes in the Netherlands, nearly ruining a world record attempt, before it was shot. A group had worked for a week to set up more than 4 million dominoes in an attempt to break the Guinness World record for falling dominoes. Last year the organizers set a new record of 4,321, 000." Where do you suppose they found all of those dominoes?

118 Marbles

Most of us still have a few marbles, maybe more than a few, tucked away in a desk or drawer. Lay down a circle of string on the floor, find a shooter—the biggest marble—as well as some smaller ones and have yourself a good time recalling how you used to practice your aim trying to move the smaller marbles out of the circle.

119 Play a musical instrument

In the past did you play the piano, clarinet, flute, drums or other musical instrument? Many of us did, but somehow through the years we lost interest, did not find time to practice or had no encouragement.

Now would be a good time to revisit those musical interests or perhaps learn to play a new instrument. Some folks have learned to play the recorder, a simple wood flute, in their later years. A recorder is inexpensive, doesn't take up much room and can be easily learned.

Playing a musical instrument has the advantage of stimulating your brain in relationship to sight, sound and touch. What a lot of circuits are lit up with making music!

120 Mimic movement

This exercise can help loosen up your thinking. Find a partner such as your spouse, a friend, a grandchild. Stand opposite from him. The idea is to copy the movement your partner makes. He may begin by raising his right hand and patting his head. Copy the movement until your partner begins a new one. Next your partner might tap his left foot with his right hand. Copy that movement, but continue doing the first one. Your partner might then shake his shoulders up and down. Copy that while continuing the two previous exercises. Then your partner makes a sound like a chicken. Mimic the sound and continue doing the previous movements. The goal is to do five movements at once. Then switch roles and begin new movements with your partner mimicking you.

This exercise is lots of fun. It shakes up old patterns of thinking and wakes up the possibilities of making new connections.

121 Table tennis as a brain sport

Daniel Amen, MD, in his recent book, *Making a Good Brain Great,* says that ping pong is the world's best brain sport. He says, "It is highly aerobic, uses both the upper and lower body, is great for eye-hand coordination and reflexes, and causes you to use many different areas of the brain at once as you are tracking the ball, planning shots and strategies."

He goes on to say that table tennis is the youngest of the world's major sports and is now recognized as an Olympic sport, making its debut in the 1988 Seoul games.

Did you ever play table tennis? Is there anyone you know who plays the game now or played in the past? Could you find a place to play now? Think about it. It would be one of the best things you could do for your brain.

THIRTEEN

television and computers: help or hindrance?

When you learned to read and write, books, pencil, pens, paper, notepads and chalkboards functioned as extensions of your brain. More recently technology such as TV and computers augments our brain's functioning. Most of us have readily adopted TV as a companion, but some of us resist using computers, which can be a boon to increasing the power of our brains. If you are using a computer, good for you. Keep on learning new ways to use it.

122 How much TV to watch

Each day for a week write down all of the TV programs you watch. Next to each listing make a note about why you watched it.

At the end of the week review what you've written. How many hours did you watch? Did you watch because there was nothing else to do? Were you using TV as an escape from reality? Do you feel better off now?

Watching television is different from reading. Reading requires you to be actively involved and sparks many parts of the brain. Did you know, according to researchers, when we're watching TV our brainwaves are much like brainwaves while asleep?

Some game shows such as Jeopardy tend to be more stimulating than soap operas. When you're watching TV, ask yourself if you're actively involved. If you're serious about optimum stimulation for your brain, here are some good programs to watch:

- Great Performances (dance, music, drama)
- Masterpiece Theater (drama)
- National Geographic specials (nature, science)
- Nova (science)
- The History Channel
- Larry King (interviews)
- Favorite sports events

123 Think

Some contend that television creates a culture in which people become consumers rather than cultivating their own creativity and making their own entertainment. Do you believe that statement is true? If you tend to agree with it, what might you do to change your own TV-watching habits? List four possibilities that feel right for you.

124 Computers and you

Computers are both wonderful and awful. Wonderful when we can send email to our families; awful when they get cranky and don't work.

When it comes to stimulation for the dendrites in our brain, we have to admit that the miracle machine gives our miracle brain a good workout.

A man works in the operations department in the central office of a large bank. Employees in the field call him when they have problems with their computers. One night, he got a call from someone in one of the branch banks who had this question: "I've got smoke coming from the back of my terminal. Do you guys have a fire downtown?"

Most of us can laugh at that question, but we often fear that we'll ask stupid questions.

We need to shake off that fear and barge ahead. Take a class to gain confidence. Keep trying new programs. Experiment. Talk computers with computer geeks.

125 If you're not intrigued with computers

What do you think or say when you listen to conversations about using computers? Do you say, "That's too complicated for me to learn" or "I'd rather spend my time reading" or "I don't have access to a computer"? Now's the time to remember that the brain research is convincing when it declares that doing new and different activities is crucial to maintaining a healthy brain.

Consider that:

- Involvement with computers may ease depression and loneliness.
- Email provides an opportunity to reconnect with old friends and distant family.
- The Internet provides financial and medical information; travel information; employment and volunteer opportunities; online shopping; an endless number of games, including bridge and chess; addresses and phone numbers.

Hopefully you're convinced and are willing to give computers a try and become computer literate. Where to start? Many senior centers and libraries and most community colleges provide learning opportunities. In some places computer tutors work with clients on their home computers or give individual lessons to residents of retirement communities, skilled nursing facilities and assisted living facilities. If you decide you want to learn, there's a way.

appendix a
answers

CHAPTER 3: Laughter Is Good for the Brain

1. **Knock-knock jokes**

    1. Goliath down. You look tired.
    2. Dewayne the bathtub. I'm drowning.
    3. Freeze a jolly good fellow, for he's . . . .
    4. Is the bell out of order? I had to knock.
    5. I butter not tell you.

2. **More knock-knocks**

    1. Amanda fix the refrigerator is here.
    2. Toby or not Toby, that is the question.
    3. Offer got my key. Let me in.
    4. Dawn by the station, early in the morning.
    5. Nunya business.
    6. Disease pants fit you?

7. **Brain teasers**

    1. Noise
    2. A nickel. The dog cost a $1.05.
    3. Just me. I'm the only one GOING to the fair.
    4. Quit imagining.
    5. Whatever color your eyes are. You're driving the bus.

8. More brain teasers

1. The catcher and umpire
2. They were married.
3. The peahen lays eggs. Peahens and peacocks are both pea fowls.
4. Eskimos live at the North Pole. Penguins live at the South Pole.
5. The surgeon was his mother.
6. Dinosaurs laid eggs long before there were chickens.

9. Like puns?

1. daisy
2. lilac
3. mimosa
4. heather
5. dahlia
6. crocus
7. poppy
8. wisteria
9. hyacinth
10. jonquil
11. zinnia

CHAPTER 5: Free Your Creativity and Imagination

38. What in the world do you know?

	1.	2.	3.	4.	5.
A	Yes	Italy	No	North	Europe
B	No	France	No	North	Europe
C	Yes	England	No	North	Europe
D	No	U.S.	Yes	North	N. America
E	Yes	Italy	No	North	Europe

CHAPTER 6: Words, words, words

42. The end's the same

1. her
2. age
3. key
4. ate
5. end
6. ten

44. Kitchen quiz

1. napkins
2. fork
3. saucepan
4. spoon
5. skillet
6. dishcloth
7. clock
8. teakettle
9. toaster
10. plates

46. Words have this in common

1. Each of these words spells another word backward. For example, "brag" spelled backward is "garb."
2. They are the first letters of common vegetables: Artichoke, mustard, lettuce, turnip, potato, asparagus, beet, onion, okra, rutabaga.

49. Run-on words

1. Home on the range.
2. IRS JFK FBI CIA
3. Roses are red violets are blue.
4. I pledge allegiance to the flag.
5. Be patient with all that is unanswered in your heart and try to love the questions.

50. Word pairs

1. plastic	11. death
2. salad	12. leave 'em
3. right	13. pencil
4. that	14. bad
5. nonsmoking	15. worse
6. swim	16. white
7. down	17. later
8. sour	18. cold
9. buy	19. blue
10. half full	20. never

51. More word pairs

1. dip	11. talk
2. flow	12. paste
3. sleep	13. Hyde
4. Barbie	14. tell
5. tired	15. dry
6. dine	16. exhale
7. match	17. bolts
8. kicking	18. socks
9. breakfast	19. potatoes
10. beans	20. sour

54. Rebuses

1. Later
2. Flag stone
3. Make a mountain out of a molehill
4. The times they are a changin'
5. Out of the blue
6. The jig is up
7. Put up or shut up
8. Lower the boom
9. Lame duck
10. The fat is in the fire
11. In one ear and out the other

55. More rebuses

1. Mixed nuts
2. The blind leading the blind
3. Reading between the lines
4. Egg on his face
5. Frog in the throat
6. Many are called, few are chosen
7. Square dance
8. Calm before the storm
9 Open and above board
10. Win hands down
11. Rally 'round the flag

56. Palindromes

1. ewe
2. dud
3. eve
4. pep
5. tat
6. eye

7. noon
8. level
9. solos
10. kayak
11. race car
12. bird rib

57. Wildflowers we love

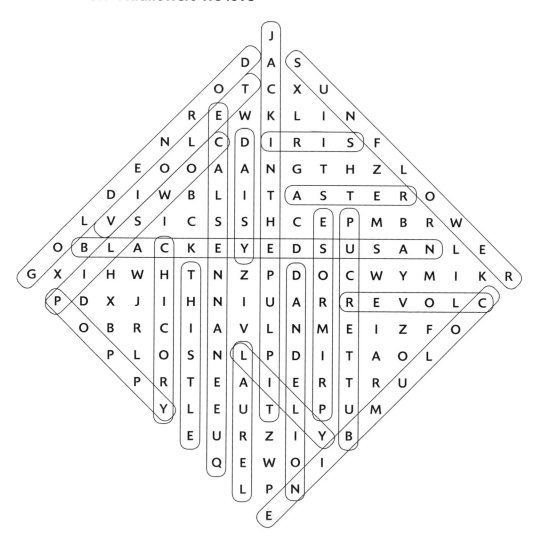

58. Word search

CHAPTER 7: Power Up Your Mind with Puzzles and Numbers

61. Sudoku

5	7	3	8	1	9	6	2	4
8	1	6	4	2	7	3	9	5
9	4	2	6	5	3	7	8	1
6	2	8	3	4	1	5	7	9
7	5	4	9	6	2	1	3	8
1	3	9	5	7	8	2	4	6
2	6	7	1	8	4	9	5	3
3	8	5	2	9	6	4	1	7
4	9	1	7	3	5	8	6	2

63. Go figure

1. $939.87

2. Chickens, ducks, turkeys

96 chickens @ $.50	$ 48
4 ducks @ $3	12
4 turkeys @ $10	40
Total	$100

64. Addition and subtraction

1. $4 + 9 + 3 + 7 - 3 - 1 = 19$
   $9 - 8 + 6 + 3 - 5 + 1 = 6$
   $3 + 5 + 3 - 9 + 6 + 5 = 13$

2.

5	6	7	8	9	**10**
61	52	63	94	46	**18**

$4 \times 4 = 16$, reverse to 61
$5 \times 5 = 25$, reverse to 52
$6 \times 6 = 36$, reverse to 63
$7 \times 7 = 49$, reverse to 94
$8 \times 8 = 64$, reverse to 46
$9 \times 9 = 81$, reverse to 18

65. Mental agility

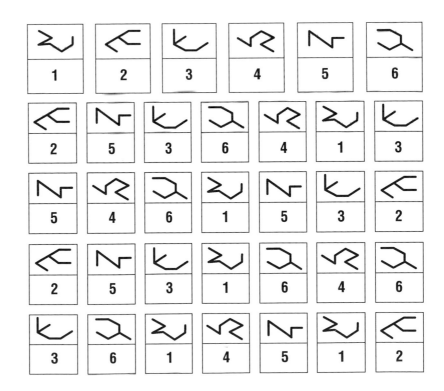

66. Toothpick puzzle

Answer: Look at 100 upside-down. Then move two toothpicks to form:

67. Walking toothpicks

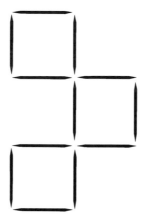

68. Tangrams

Here are some ideas of shapes to create.

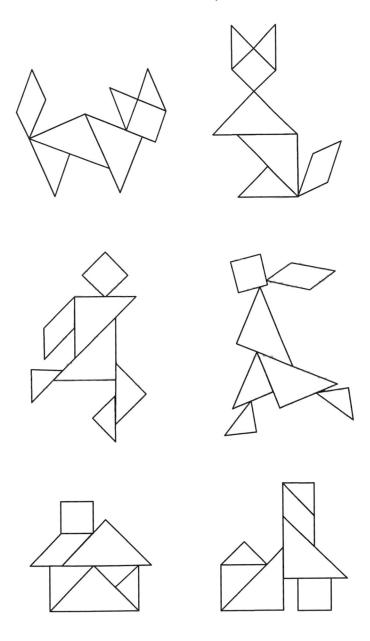

CHAPTER 9: Have Fun with Visual Arts and Illusions

85. Draw a pig

If the pig is drawn:

- Toward the top of the paper, you're positive and optimistic.
- Toward the middle, you're a realist.
- Toward the bottom, you're pessimistic and have a tendency to behave negatively.
- Facing left, you believe in tradition, are friendly and remember dates (birthdays, etc.).
- Facing right, you're innovative and active but don't have a strong sense of family, nor do you remember dates.
- Facing front (looking at you), you are direct, enjoy playing devil's advocate and neither fear nor avoid discussions.
- With many details, you're analytical, cautious and distrustful.
- With few details, you are emotional and naive, care little for details and enjoy taking risks.
- With less than four legs showing, you are insecure or are living through a period of major change.
- With four legs showing, you're secure, stubborn, and idealistic.
- The size of the ears indicates how good a listener you are. The bigger the better.

There's no need to take this too seriously. It may not be very accurate for you. There are pigs and there are pigs.

CHAPTER 10: Build Your Spatial Abilities

91. Tile designs

1 matches C and 4 matches A.

92. Fun with diagrams and figures

1. Figure F is the only one that doesn't contain a triangle.
2. Figure A is the only figure without a straight line.
3. Figure D omits the horizontal line as it was omitted in the circle.

93. Pencils and more pencils

There are three different lengths and four pencils of each length:

Short   a, f, h, i
Medium   b, e, j, l
Long   c, d, g, k

94. Bottle caps

The following cap in the second picture is not in the first picture.

95. Name that state

96. States that end with the letter A

Twenty-one states end with A:

Alabama	Nebraska
Alaska	Nevada
Arizona	North Carolina
California	North Dakota
Florida	Oklahoma
Georgia	Pennsylvania
Indiana	South Carolina
Iowa	South Dakota
Louisiana	Virginia
Minnesota	West Virginia
Montana	

CHAPTER 11: Remember When

108. Remembering

1. Cheese: Velveeta, cheddar, bleu cheese, feta, Provolone, Swiss, Lindberger, Muenster, farmer cheese, Gouda, brick, Colby, Edam, Monterey Jack, etc.
2. Cars: Ford, Pontiac, Mercedes Benz, Volkswagen, Honda, BMW, Toyota, Buick, Dodge, Lincoln, Mercury, Plymouth, Fiat, Audi, Cadillac, Jeep, Oldsmobile, Chrysler, Rolls Royce, Chevrolet, Volvo, Mazda, etc.
3. Birds: Crow, robin, sparrow, purple finch, house finch, chickadee, nuthatch, cardinal, blue jay, blue bird, red wing blackbird, junco, sandhill crane, whooping crane, starling, purple grackle, turkey, hawk, owl, etc.
4. Trees: Maple, elm, spruce, pine, cherry, peach, plum, apricot, ginko, service berry, walnut, ash, hickory, weeping willow, birch, oak, poplar, box elder, etc.

110. Little remembered facts about presidents

1. Hoover (10)
2. Jefferson (3)
3. Reagan (11)
4. Johnson (9)
5. Eisenhower (12)
6. Lincoln (4)
7. George W. Bush (5)
8. Washington (7)
9. Franklin Roosevelt (8)
10. Clinton (6)
11. Carter (2)
12. Truman (1)

appendix b
resources

Books

Adams, Patch. *Gesundheit*. Rochester, VT: Healing Arts, 1998.

Amen, Daniel. *Making a Good Brain Great*. Easton, PA: Harmony Books, 2005.

Acherman, Diane. *A Natural History of the Senses*. New York: Vintage Books, 1990.

Block, J. Richard, and Harold Yuker. *Can You Believe Your Eyes?* New York: Gardener Press, 1989.

Bortz, Walter M. II. *Dare to Be 100*. New York: Simon and Shuster, 1996.

Boterman, Jack, and Heleen Tichler. *The Big Brain Workout*. New York: Sterling, 2005.

Carper, Jean, *Your Miracle Brain*. Quill Edition. New York: Harpers Collins, 2001.

Cohen, Gene. *The Creative Age: Awakening Human Potential in the Second Half of Life*. New York: Avon, 2000.

Crawford, Chris. *Tangram Puzzles: 500 Tricky Shapes to Confound and Astound*. New York: Sterling, 2002.

Cusack, Sandra, and Wendy Thompson. *Mental Fitness For Life: Seven Steps to Healthy Aging.* Toronto: Key Porter, 2003.

Davis, Gary A. *Creativity Is Forever.* Dubuque, IA: Kendall Hunt, 1992.

Ellis, Neenah. *If I Live to Be 100, Lessons from the Centenarians.* New York: Three River Press, 2004.

Engelman, Marge. *Aerobics of the Mind* (revised ed.). Verona, WI: Attainment, 2006.

Engelman, Marge. *Aerobics of the Mind: Mental Fitness Cards.* Verona, WI: Attainment, 2001.

Gamon, David, and Allen D. Bragdon, *Building Mental Muscle.* New York: Barnes and Noble, 1998.

Gediman, Corinne L, with Francis M. Crinella. *Brainfit.* Nashville, TN: Rutledge Hill, 2005.

Gelb, Michael J. *How To Think Like Leonardo Da Vinci.* New York: Dell, 1998.

Isaksen, Scott C., and Donald J. Treffinger. *Workbook for Creative Problem Solving: The Basic Course.* Buffalo, NY: Berly, 1985.

Katz, Lawrence B., and Manning Rubin. *Keep Your Brain Alive.* New York: Workman, 1999.

LasCola, Amy (Ed.). *Brain Teasers, Critical Thinking Activities.* Huntington Beach, CA: Teacher Created Materials, 1993.

Lee, James L., and Charles J. Pulvino. *Educating the Forgotten Half.* Dubuque, IA: Kendall/Hunt, 1992.

Lewthwaite, Nancy J. *A Resource Manual of Mentally Stimulating Group Activities.* Victoria, BC: Author, 1992.

Long, Jill Murphy. *Permission to Play.* Naperville, IL: Sourcebook, 2003.

Lustrabader, Wendy. *What's Worth Knowing*. New York: Jeremy Tarcher, 2001.

Making the Most of Your Brain: How to Use Your Mind to Improve Your Life. London: Reader's Digest Association, 2002.

Noir, Michel, and Bernard Croisile. *Dental Floss for the Mind: A Complete Program for Boosting Your Brain Power*. New York: McGraw-Hill, 2005.

Parnes, Sidney J., Ruth G. Noller, and Angelo M. Biondi. *Guide to Creative Action*. Creative Education Foundation. New York: Scribner's, 1977.

Perls, Thomas, and Margery Hunter-Silvers. *Living to 100*. New York: Basic Books, 1989.

Ratey, John J. *A User's Guide to the Brain*. New York: Vintage Books, 2002.

Restak, Richard. *Mozart's Brain and the Fighter Pilot: Unleashing Your Brain Potential*. New York: Harmony Books, 2001.

Scott, Willard. *The Older the Fiddle the Better the Tune*. New York: Hyperion, 2003.

Seagull, Beatrice, and Sara Seagull. *Mind Your Mind: A Whole Brain Workout for Older Adults*. Verona, WI: Attainment, 2004.

Short, Cynthia S. *Grow Dendrites Forever: The Brain Fitness Kit*. Lakeside, MT: Author, 1998.

Shortz, Will (presenter). *Sudoku*. New York: St. Martin's Griffin, 2005.

Tharp, Twyla. *The Creative Habit: Learn It and Use It for Life*. New York: Simon and Shuster, 2003.

Weaver, Frances. *The Girls with Grandmother Faces: A Celebration of Life's Potential for Those Over 55*. New York: Hyperion, 1996.

Winter, Arthur, and Ruth Winter. *Brain Workout*. New York: St. Martin's Griffin, 1997.

Flash Cards

U.S. Presidents: Pocket Flash Cards. St. Paul, MN: Trend Enterprises, 2001.

Papers

Schaie, K. Warner, and Sherry L. Willis. "Intellectual Functioning in Adulthood: Growth, Maintenance, Decline, and Modifiability." Presented to the American Society on Aging annual meeting, 2005.

White House Conference on Aging. Washington, DC, May 1995.

Periodicals and Newsletters

The Brain in the News. Reprints of news stories from United States' leading newspapers. New York: Charles Dana Foundation. Bimonthly issues 1998–2005.

Harvard Health Letter, December 2001.

Journal of the American Medical Association, September 22, 2004.

PositScience, Winter 2005–06.

Rosenfeld, Isadore. "Health on Parade." *Parade Magazine*, January 15, 2006.

Vos Savant, Marilyn. "Ask Marilyn." *Parade Magazine*, various issues 2003–05.

Suhren, Linda, *WOW! Wondrously Older and Wiser,* 2002.

Websites

New internet resources are coming on line every day. You'll find information on every possible subject. Listed here are a few that have special value for older adults. Other internet resources are listed with specific exercises in the book.

www.aarp.org/internetresources Here you'll find descriptions of and links to over 700 of the best websites for older adults, arranged by topic. Search or browse 11 topic areas. Updated regularly. One of the topic areas is Leisure Learning and Personal Growth—a rich resource of mental fitness activities.

www. aarpmagazine.org/games This is a more direct resource where you'll find crossword puzzles, jumbles, universal trivia, jigsaw puzzles, word search and rootonymn (complete the missing word).

www.happyneuron.com It's billed as the "premier mental fitness program." Daily brain teasers, Sudoku puzzles, trivia quizzes, word search, jigsaw puzzles and IQ tests. It's updated six days a week.

http://www.positscience.com/science/ Posit Science Brain Fitness program, based around "brain training" computer exercises.

http://www/asaging.org.cdc American Society on Aging's "Strategies for Cognitive Vitality," a free downloadable curriculum on cognitive wellness.

http://www.aarp.org/nrta Dana Alliance for Brain Health and AARP's "Staying Sharp" campaign, which includes live presentations, a website, TV broadcasts and print materials.